Taken by the Eagle

Stella Longland

a Cave of Clay book

Copyright © Stella Longland 2020

Cover design by Stella Longland ©

first edition

All rights reserved. No part of this publication may be reproduced, stored in a retrieval system, or transmitted in any form or by any means without prior written permission of the copyright owner. Nor can it be circulated in any form of binding or cover other than that in which it is published and without similar condition including this condition being imposed on a subsequent purchaser.

British Library Cataloguing in Publication Data
A catalogue record for this book is available from the British Library

ISBN 978-1-9999024-4-5

What is the Power?
All of the Mystery of the in-coming.

What is a Spirit?
The Mystery has taken on a form.

Thank you
Joseph, Beautiful Painted Arrow,
for the help you have given me
and for the healings I receive from
the Teachings you have given to us all.

*This story was written
from the texts of audio tapes
recorded in a state of consciousness somewhere between
the worlds out there and the world of every day.*

Consult the final 7 pages to find
    About Sixteen Years
    About the Medicine Sphere
    About Dancing Light
    About Drawing a Line
    Other Books by the Author
    Index pages

Contents:

Divine Longing

A-ah
Feathers
Flowers of the Rainbow
Offering Myself

E-eh
The Heart Centre
The Fisher
At the Red Rock

I-ii
Houses to Live in
Encountering the Power
The Eagle's Body
A House to Live In

O-oh
Being of Thunder
Becoming the Power
The Heart of the Father
Be As You Are

U-uu
Standing Together
The Rainbow
Time Steps
The Colour Yellow

What is the medicine wheel?
A map of the territory.

sounds of the 5 directions

Divine Longing

One day, on impulse, I decided to go to a local stone circle that I had visited once before after finding it marked on the ordnance survey map. This circle, how ancient I do not know, is made by sixteen small stones, all about one foot tall, set in a ring twenty feet in diameter. It sits on a west facing hillside in a field of rough upland pasture.

Standing outside the circle looking across to the West, I felt inspired to create a medicine wheel ceremony. Creating a ceremony is, for me, a way to say thank you to Life and to seek help in my life.

Going by the position of the Sun, I chose the stone on my left as the East point. Crouching down and cupping my hands around it I sang, in the way my Teacher had recently taught me, the sound of the East: "-ah" and I prayed: "I don't want to just live and die. I want to ....., I want to do something ....., I want to do something to .....," but I was unable to find the words to express my desire. I walked on, clockwise round the outside of the circle, to reach the South. Crouching down and holding the stone, I sang: "-eh" and cried out: "Please, help me!" Continuing the circuit, I went to the West stone, and, bending to touch it, I sang: "-ii." No need to say any words; the stone was aware. I walked to the North and, touching that stone, sang: "-oh." The medicine wheel was alive.

The wind was blowing from the North. When I asked for help in the South it was blowing into my face bringing help to me. When I stood at the North it was blowing on my back encouraging me to move forwards. I walked into the circle through the North and went to the centre. I raised my arms not confidently at first because there was a farmer rounding up sheep a few fields away, then confidently, with arms raised, asking to connect to above and below, I sang: "-uu" and while I sang I bent down and touched the ground. Then I stood up. I walked an inner circuit of the stones and, to finish the ceremony, when I was by the North stone again, I stepped out of the circle backwards.

I headed off across the Fell. I decided to walk along the back of the wood, some way below the ridge of the hillside, to the place where I know that a spring rises. As I walked, I came across a flat-topped stone with a cup-shaped depression in the surface which was full of clear water. I took some of that water and sprinkled it onto my head, took some more and touched my throat, and with a few more drops I patted my heart. Feeling very light, I went on to where the spring bursts out from under a great grey stone weighing many tons. I stood facing the stone, the shallow, bubbling water washing over my feet, and I heard a bird calling.

The cry came from one of the birds of prey that hunt along the ridge. It was circling above the wood, above me, shrieking sharp short cries, calling, calling; calling to me. Longing to be up there with that bird, closed my eyes. When I opened them and looked up again, two birds were flying there. Calling out, they circled in opposite directions nearly touching each other as they passed but not quite. For a long time, I watched them; filled with a longing that was still without words.

When the time came, I walked down the side of the wood and, crossing over the dry-stone wall into the lane, I made my way towards my parked car. As I passed beneath a big Ash tree, I felt its magnetic power and it spoke to me in my mind asking me what it was that I wanted. "That's a difficult question." I said and walked on thinking about it. I knew I must say something. I knew that, however passionate, longing without expression is no help. I realized, if I wanted help to arrive, I had to formulate an answer before I got to the next big tree. I reached the next big tree and I said: "I want to do something to contribute to taking better care of the planet." The tree listened deeply and replied: "What could that be?"

I walked on thoughtfully; I had written on the comment form of the seminar I had recently attended how I would go home and try to drop subtle hints to people that the spirit world might exist and be beneficial in their lives. So that is what I told the third big tree, but the only thing I was sure of was that, when the big birds were crying and flying together in the sky, I felt an overwhelming longing for something.....

Feathers

I will record this because I am not able to remember these altered state experiences for long and I don't see how I can make any progress if I can't hold on to the memories. Lying down and letting my awareness of my physical body fade, and after passing through various changes of state, I saw a circular shield with three large feathers hanging on it. The shield was covered in brown skin; the feathers were white but the one on the right had a black mark on it. The shield was hanging on crossed lances.

3 feathers on a shield

I moved very close to the shield and, when I touched it, I felt a prickling sensation all over my body. Then the shield went very far away and I couldn't reach it, but I caught a glimpse of yellow on the right-hand side and, when I concentrated on that, I rose rapidly towards the sky where all I could see was a vivid yellow colour.

My field of vision was filled with a very small part of a very large foot, the left foot of an immense bird, I was like a speck of dust beside it; it belonged to an Eagle. I caught a glimpse of a glittering left eye, but I couldn't assemble a complete picture. I was wondering: "Is this Eagle going to do something?" But no, it stood there, rock solid. There was nothing to be done. I thought about the colour Yellow: on the medicine wheel, it is the colour of the East and through the gate of that direction, the breath of Life enters the wheel. That was important: a memory established if you like.

I attended a seven-day residential seminar, on the mysteries of sound and light, under the guidance of my Teacher, Alexander. During the week he suggested we have a free evening to relax and process our work. I went to the beach. I lay on a flat bed of sandstone looking towards the sunset; there were broken clouds around the Sun and their edges were gold, in among them there was a long stretch of blue sky. Slowly it became a visionary experience and I travelled there. The valley floor was blue sky and the cloud hills were gold; through the valley ran a glacial river and snow-covered mountains towered on either side.

On returning, I stared up at the sky directly above my face. There were fluffy banks of very small white clouds which were all a similar size and shape; they seemed like a host of living creatures and behind them was the penetrating blue sky. I noticed I had two distinct layers of vision, both of which were in perfect focus. I could see all the floaters in my eyes like a cobweb structure across my vision and beyond that web, the amazing living blue and the host of white Beings which were pressing down on me. The sight was so extraordinary that I went, through the cobweb, away into the blueness in a most strange, strange way.

The Sun set and the colours faded. I got up and, walking back along the beach, I began to pick up feathers that combined both black and white. In the afternoon my Teacher had talked so brilliantly about the Black and the White Lights that this inspired me to notice black and white feathers and to collect them. As I was combing along the tide line among the heaps of debris, I saw the remains of a very large feather. It was the longest feather I had ever seen, and I picked it out from all the rubbish lying there. The white spine measured sixteen inches but less than an inch of the stiff black barbs was left at the top. The next morning, I showed it to my Teacher; my joke feather that I felt very serious about. He thought it might be an Eagle's feather. That was great. I had found it. It was mine.

Later that morning we did past life work. The group split into pairs: one would travel, and one would listen and ask questions. The person I paired up with would travel first. I suggested to him that he lie down and relax very deeply and we stayed there, very quiet, while everybody else settled down. I was looking at him lying there and I saw a beautiful feather covering him. The quill point was lying on his forehead and the feather ran right down his body. The spine of the feather was entirely white, and the soft silky barbs were reddish brown where they attached to the spine merging to white at their outer ends. It lay over him and covered him like a blanket. It looked wonderful, and warm yellow light was shining there. I was happy. In his journey, he had the most fabulous memory back to a life in the Arctic. I enjoyed his story. Not only was it interesting for me to listen to, it was a deeply happy experience for him. Then it was my turn. I lay under the same feather.

As I entered the altered state, everything was brown. I travelled down a brown tunnel, and I arrived in a brown place; a conical shelter covered with skins. Everything around me was brown except for a couple of splashes of the colour white. Slowly these two colours formed into the image of an Eagle. The feathers were brown; the feet, the beak and part of the face around it, were white.

The Eagle was perched on a T-shaped wooden stand, but it was not alive, it was a totem and I was standing before it. I was a young woman old enough to have children. I had clothes and shoes made of brown skins; everything was brown except the white face, beak and feet of the Eagle. I was aware of people standing behind me. They stood quietly while the Eagle and I made contact and it was the most wonderful feeling. Starting on the backs of my hands, in my feet, and in my legs the essence of the connection with the Eagle got stronger and stronger until it filled my whole body.

My partner asked me what was happening, and I said: "I am getting a gift." He said: "What is it?" and I replied: "Connection." He asked me what I was going to do with the gift in the future and I said: "I don't know." But I was ready, and I had a feeling that I would be asked to do things when necessary and that I would do them. As my partner asked me questions, I knew that the spiritual process would continue and not be interrupted, so I left the Eagle's gift to fill me up and answered him as best I could. He asked me about the people with me. I couldn't say much, but we loved each other. I didn't find it necessary to know more. I had two things to do: receive the gift and tell my partner in the exercise what was happening. The second was quite hard, but I knew that the gift wasn't only mine; I had to pass it on, and that is what I did.

When I came back, I felt very sad. A tear ran down my face because I felt the kind of changes that I feel as I come back in from a deep spirit place; the return of the feelings of being in a physical body that were lost without my noticing as I went out; feeling the reality of the vision diminishing, diminishing and diminishing, until it is only a memory, and it is hard. It is hard, but it is worth it. The particular nature of the re-entry problem on this occasion made me think that this was not a past life experience but a visit to a spirit place.

The seminar ended and I returned to work, running my soft furnishing business, with many experiences to integrate into my daily life. One particular morning when I got up, the Moon was full and brilliantly shining at six a.m. with a greenish silver light. I lay down to meditate and, not able to connect to anything, wandered. I wandered, and white was there, it brought me to the white face of the Eagle in the lodge. I stayed looking at that Eagle for a long time, till, perhaps as a result of double vision caused by staring, the T-shaped stand became the shape of a trilithon.

T   π

T and Trilithon

It looked like an entrance and maybe I could walk through, but I hesitated and suddenly the sofa cover we made in the workshop recently came, baff, into my mind. When I put it on the sofa the pleat was a bad fit because the material the customer supplied had been washed, so when it was sewn it had stretched, technical details, and the pleat was all wobbly and hung badly.

This problem came, baff, like that into the forefront of my experience and it had to be sorted through. Should I deliver the cover as it was and hope the customer would not notice, or should I alter it? It was incredibly important that I made a decision, a spiritual decision if you like, about it at that very moment. I needed to state: "I will alter it today." And that was so hard. I looked and looked for a way out. Then, when it seemed that it was inevitable that I should alter it, I looked and looked at the monetary aspect of it. Who should pay? Why should it be me who paid? What were the moral issues? The customer could afford it, but they relied on my expertise to do the best job at a reasonable price using my knowledge to achieve this. But it was not me who made the mistake. It was my employee because she was inexperienced, and I did not keep an eye on her. I had had a moment of laziness and wanted out of the everlasting attention to minute details that my job requires, for what? for money? It takes all the energy I have got and gives me some money in return!

Oh dear, I was upset that this came and broke my connection, but I knew perfectly well that the work of this world has to be right for the other world work to be right also. I cannot behave without good intent here and hope to make progress there. Hum, I just want to travel and enjoy myself, and not be presented with these challenges! So, after the seminar, a traumatic time: painful.

Last night my partner and I watched a programme on the formation of rocks and afterwards he started, you could call it a discussion, but he launched an attack on me about spirituality. He said: "It's all chemistry and where does spirituality suddenly arrive from?" I tried to talk to him but most of the time he could not listen; he wanted to domineer. He told me that I had got religion and that I was mad. It was not particularly acrimonious, but it was extremely stressful, so when I went to bed, I had terrible pain in my heart and wanted to weep. I meditated, the pain went away, and I felt calm. In the night I woke up and a very strong spiritual force was present. I drank that in as much as I could. I remembered what my Teacher said, in his most recent letter, about how the Spirit, who guides his Teacher Joseph, came to me in the seminar. I thought: "I have always wondered about this beautiful incoming Spirit, so that is who it is!" and I decided that I would always accept the spiritual guidance from that source, and I felt very happy to be part of it.

I slept very well, but this morning when I woke up my heart pain came back. I felt I must meditate upon it. The journey started: all the past was a huge black mound of impenetrable stuff which impelled me forward. It built itself without my volition and, in that way, it raised me up towards the future.

I felt myself becoming a bird taking flight. I wondered: "What kind of bird is this?" As I flew, I entered a tunnel. I recognised it as the tunnel which I went down to meet the Eagle. I flew down that tunnel and arrived at that perch and sat on that perch. I wondered: "Am I alive or dead? It was a dead Eagle which perched here before, so what state am I in?" And: "How come I am in this Eagle?"

Sitting on the perch I looked out of Eagle's eyes. I looked down and I saw myself standing there as I was when I first came into that place, a young woman. I called to myself and myself came to me and we became one in the heart centre. I returned and, as I came back, I felt all the changes right to the time when I re-emerged in the pain in my heart. I was sad to come back and I thought: "Why does that pain need to be there?" But it does. And I carry on from here.

I was travelling horizontally when I saw a group of conical shelters placed in a circle. I entered this circle and standing before a particular shelter I felt great love in my heart. The skin cover split vertically to make an entrance and I went through into the circular space of the interior. Immediately I saw the totem Eagle, and, through the Eagle, I went into the T-shaped stand. The Eagle became an emblem hanging on the stand, suspended on my chest. I bent my head forward to kiss this emblem but instead I swallowed it. Once inside me the emblem turned over and spread out within to become an Eagle again. The most joyful and magnificent feeling filled me as I realized that, by entering the circle of the shelter and becoming the T-shaped stand, a symbol had been created which, somewhere along the line, is very familiar to me, a T inside an O, an emblem which carries the medicine of the Eagle.

a familiar symbol

Flowers of the Rainbow

Last night watching television with my partner I suffered from arrested heart beats and I couldn't control them so, at ten o'clock, I came to bed and meditated. I shut my eyes and the enormous eye of a bird was there. We had been watching a documentary on birds and no doubt that focused this image. I stuck with it and, passing through the barrier, I arrived on a bare grey-brown mountain plateau. I soon knew that the plateau was the brown feathers of the Eagle's back and to the left there was a snow-covered mountain which was the Eagle's head. I bent down and touched the hard feather surface of this magnificent bird. The Eagle's feathers are stiff, resilient and very strong.

After a while a Black Spirit came and I was frightened. I was afraid on the first occasion that I had seen and felt the power of this Being. I was afraid now. I was most afraid of the strength of my own feelings of attraction to it. But I overcame my fear and allowed the feeling of this Being to come into my mind. I became very calm and my heart palpitations went away. I let myself go away, safe in the power of something much, much greater than me.

This morning, meditating, I went straight back to that plateau.

Standing there I felt I should give everything I had energy-wise to the still, stone-like mountain bird, and I did this by lying face down on the brown ground, opening my energy centres and sending all I could to the Eagle. When that was done, a tall tree grew. I looked up and the branches of this tree were silhouetted against the blue sky; the tree had grown great on the plateau of the Eagle's back. So, during the coming seminar, when I meditate and I go travelling, the Eagle will come bringing some mighty visualisation of its body.

One evening during the seminar we took a shamanic journey to the upper world supported in our travelling by music on a cd instead of, the more usual method, to the regular beat of a drum. The opening instructions for a journey to the upper world are to climb a mountain and travel through clouds.

Immediately the music started everything was black, beautiful shiny black. I saw the tallest pitch-black mountain with steep sides and a snow-capped peak. Directly above the mountain a star shone in the night sky so that the star appeared to rest upon the snowy top. I drifted towards them; it was deep night and the sides of the mountain stretched up, merging into the sky, but that did not daunt me. I was in a very happy state of mind and in the mood for some fun. I wanted to take all my totem creatures with me to the upper world and so I decided to call them.

The Black Coyote and the Yellow Coyote came at once, and then I called the others. I started in the root centre, and I called to the Rocks. I moved to the centre of generation, and I called to the Trees. I moved to the solar plexus, and I called the Owl. I moved to the heart centre, and I called the Deer. As they came, one after the other, I felt really proud.

When they were all present, I pointed to the Star and said: "We are all going there. We will travel as a rocket; that is how we will travel." The Tree said: "I can make a rocket ship." The Tree would make the rocket ship out of its body. The Stones said: "With the energy that is locked into us, we will make the fuel to drive the rocket." The Owl offered to be the stabilisers. The Deer said: "With my horns, I will be the directional navigation system." The rocket ship began to take shape. The Black Coyote said: "I will be all the space that we have to travel through because I am the sum of all your incarnations so far and that makes the space that you have for your mind to play in." The Yellow Coyote would be the nose cone of the rocket; the part that gives it the inspiration to go.

We were ready to go, and we went. But as we penetrated the outer atmosphere, which must be the required clouds, we realized that the Stones had expended their energy in the launch, fragmenting their bodies to dust, and they were left behind. When we left the outer atmosphere, the rocket ship, which was the Tree, fell apart and was left behind. I felt distraught that I had to leave these beloved things behind, but I was fierce with myself: "Keep it together!" We circled the Earth a few times and we looked down at it, blue and white. I said to the others: "Let's get it together. We have to go on now in the new vehicle that we have become."

This new vehicle was extremely strange. The horns of the Deer spiralled around each other and the colour black from the Black Coyote became one spiral and the colour yellow from the Yellow Coyote became the other spiral. The wings of the Owl remained to set our trajectory, and the two eyes of the Owl were stuck on the ends of the two spiral strands. They were my eyes, and that is how we travelled through the outer space-ness of it all.

Once the direction was set, it became clear that the brown wings of the Owl were no longer appropriate for the environment, and they fell off. Then there was just the double spiral; the black strand and the yellow strand, and the two eyes; yellow eyes with black centres, travelling through space; rolling, rolling through space with the spiral energy, beautifully orientated on the target, no problem at all.

We arrived at the top of the Mountain and entered the Star. After a little while spent getting used to this new environment, I realized that the Star was an enormous faceted diamond. I could see some of the colours of the spectrum playing on the faces of this diamond; red, green, and blue. I seemed to have lost my black and yellow spiral body; when I tried to visualize it, it did not fit in that place at all. I knew I had achieved my goal and I entered a state of bliss.

But, all too soon, it was a bliss with an element of discontent because I felt purposeless and I thought: "Is this it? Is this what I sacrificed the Trees and Stones for?" I didn't despair, I just thought: "Oh, is this all, to be inside a massive diamond in a state of suspended animation?" This diamond existence went on for quite a while. I decided: "I will just have to accept it. I integrated the two Coyotes, and this is where I ended up."

Slowly, imperceptibly slowly, I became an oval-shaped bed of freshly dug brown earth located somewhere. A rainbow appeared. I was a flower bed, and I could grow those rainbow colours into flowers. Red, a single Tulip appeared. Orange, a Marigold sprang up. Yellow, a Buttercup flowered. Green, some Moss appeared. Blue, a Bluebell. Indigo, a Primula, and Violet was a Violet. That was very beautiful, very simple, very straightforward, and I felt fulfilled. With surprise I noticed that I was crying. I thought: "That's weird there are tears running out of my right eye, but am I sad?"

Suddenly a huge yellow eye was staring at me; an Eagle, its head cocked on one side, its right eye very close to the ground, was looking straight at me. It struck into the ground with its beak and picked me up. As the Eagle swallowed me, I caught a glimpse of myself: I was an earthworm. The music stopped, and the seminar leader said: "Come back."

7 flowers of the rainbow

The journey was over and now I must confess that when we arrived at the Star I was aware of the insubstantial form of a silver-white Being who came towards me, seeming to want to make contact and indicating that I should follow it, but I thought it was a spaceman, or a Being from another planet; I did not want to take a sci-fi journey and I would not go. I have to confess this now because later in this story I will meet that Being again.

After the seminar I left for home on the same day as my Teacher went to teach abroad. I took him to the airport. After we parted I drove into the strangest weather. It had been a bright sunny day, suddenly it was black as night to my left and intense, blinding sunlight to my right. The most amazing double rainbow appeared; at first it was single then another joined it a few miles further on. The inner rainbow had red on the outer arc, the outer rainbow had red on the inner arc. The colours so vibrant and so brilliant against the storm cloud, it was a fantastic awe-inspiring sight.

Given that during the seminar I was an earthworm, well, in fact, since I had been eaten by the Eagle, an ex-earthworm, I decided to change my attitude in meditation and allow myself to be taken even if it would mean losing ninety per cent of the contents.

Offering Myself

As I travelled round the medicine wheel, I became aware of myself as earth and the Eagle standing above me. I opened my body from top to bottom; pealing the edges back to reveal the earthworm within. The Eagle looked up and down the furrow and, bending its head forward, pushed its beak into my chest only interested in my heart centre; as a result, blue and yellow were infused into my heart. Then the Eagle rolled my heart as if it was an egg and settled down to incubate this egg. We stayed in a very quiet and thoughtless state until it was time to return. On the return, I thought: "It is spring, and all the birds are nesting now."

This morning the Eagle came again and filled my Being, very slowly, very carefully, from the top down. I did not become the Eagle; the Eagle infused me. In return, I opened up my bodies and I showed the Eagle the dark corners and the places where my motivations are not pure. It was painful and I cried but I searched to find them all. It was in the area of my solar plexus and my heart that I found those hidden crannies, and I showed them all to the Eagle.

The Eagle became more en-wrapping of me and this went on till three quarters of an hour had gone by. During that time, the Eagle took me up into the pure colour of a translucent blue sky, a sky that I have seen in glimpses of a crystal-clear world which lies beyond the world of nature that I inhabit, the Blue was intense and everything else withdrew.

When I left the Above, which I had to do because, being the Being that I am, I cannot be there entirely, I became aware and, feeling myself sinking into the dark earth, I was disheartened, but as soon as I was engulfed by the Earth a whole set of different ecstatic feelings arose in me and the disappointment that I experienced was translated into exquisite joy. Then, through my centre of generation, the secret, crystal-clear world, which lies beyond, flooded into my perception and I realized it is in the centre of generation that the Blue of Above meets the Green of Below and they join together there. I allowed the visions of that hidden world to come into me and that was amazing beyond belief.

In the Eagle my higher centres are my focus, in the other realm I focus in my lower centres, and I had a clear perception of how both places contain ecstasy. The Eagle will take me Above and the Spirit of the Earth will take me Below: the ecstasy of one is equal to the ecstasy of the other. I am able to move between these states because that is the experience of Being in this life.

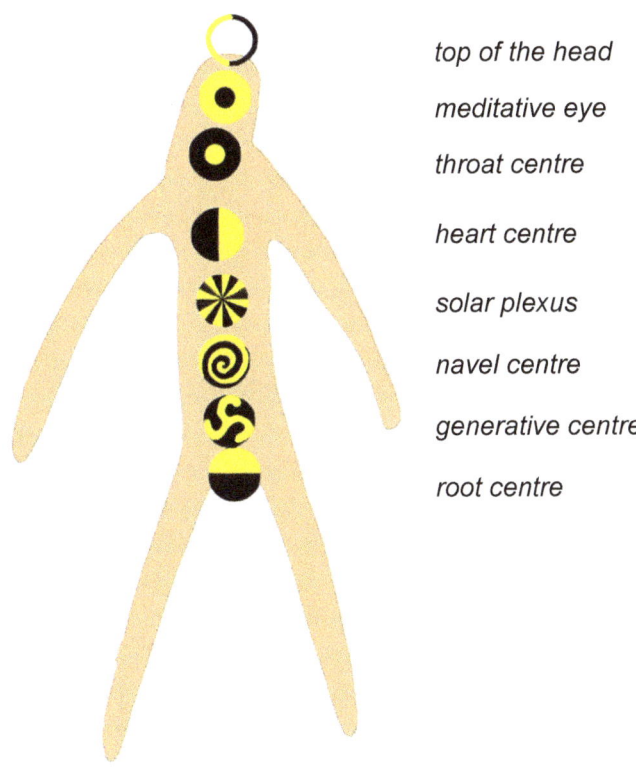

top of the head

meditative eye

throat centre

heart centre

solar plexus

navel centre

generative centre

root centre

8 energy centres

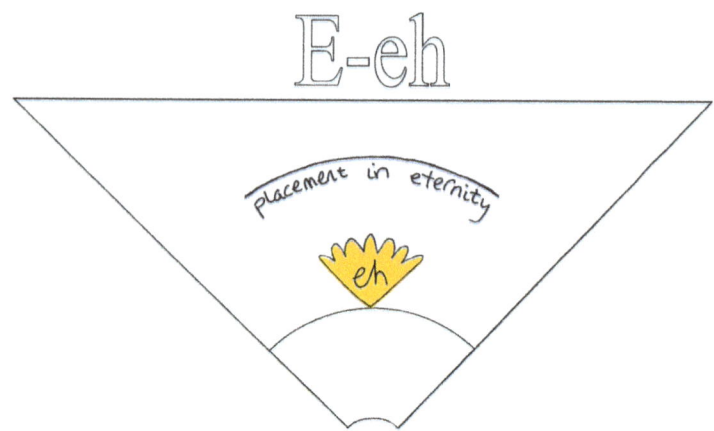

The Heart Centre

Last night I tried something new; to go consciously and find something out, something, anything, that I did not already know. First, I tried to go to my two human Teachers, my Teacher in Scotland and his Teacher in America, and I connected strongly into images of them both. Then I saw an image that was like shiny black feathers. I thought I was looking at an Eagle which was also a person with the name 'Black Eagle', and it all struck me as very silly. I was sceptical, not sure if I was making everything up, and I withdrew.

I am having a crisis in my daily life at the moment; I am getting ready to participate in my first ceremonial dance, a ceremony received in vision by my Teacher's Teacher, Joseph Rael, Beautiful Painted Arrow, with the instruction to give it to all races, and I am trying to organize my working life so that everything will go smoothly there and here. The process has been causing me some disturbance, turmoil, and confusion.

Eventually I organised all the aspects of my complicated life and I made it to the first Sun Moon Dance to be danced in England, a dry fasting ceremony taking place over four days. On the third day I broke through the pain and sickness and began to discover levels of Beauty. As each dance started, I would hear a word and I would dance in honour of that word, forwards and backwards, to and from, the Y-shaped Tree placed in the centre of the dance arbour.

The first word was 'Tolerance'. In the next dance the word was 'Peace'. As I was dancing Peace, I saw, in my inner vision, a vertical crack appear in the Tree. This crack opened wide. I was dancing wrapped in a blanket because the day had started off chilly. Suddenly I was very hot. I went to my place and threw the blanket off, returning to the spot where I had been before and looking intently at this crack. Holding on, or maybe I was holding off, I debated internally: "Will I go now, or will I wait, maybe even until tomorrow, pushing the limits?" Suddenly a voice behind me said: "Are you going to go?" I said: "I am" and threw myself at the Tree, for a moment my arms encircled it, then, letting go, I fell backwards onto the ground.

They picked me up carried me to my resting place, the Chief touched my solar plexus with an Eagle's wing, it was strong, resilient, and my energy reached outwards in response to the touch. They left me and I experienced Peace. That was the gift that was given to me then. I understood what Peace felt like and why it would be so wonderful if all people could find Peace.

In the next dance I danced 'Happiness'. Then I danced in praise of power animals. It may have been then that the european Buzzard soared above and floated motionless between the two branches of the Y-shaped Tree. In the rest period between this and the next dance I felt the Buffalo enter me from the base up. It rose until it filled me and came to rest in my heart. Then the Eagle came into my head and round my head and was my head. I understood that it was given to me that I could dance the next dance in honour of the Buffalo and the Eagle. I did that. I danced the Buffalo to a certain point towards the Tree and then I danced the Eagle from there on in. This turned out to be the last dance of the day.

I felt very tired when we got up to dance on the fourth day, but I think my energy would have returned. We had done two or three dances when, as I danced, I heard this: "Till the end of Time." I understood that this kind of ceremonial dance, which enables communication between incarnate and discarnate Beings, would continue until the end of Time and, also, that I would be there, dancing.

Returning home, calmer than before, I resumed my working life. I woke one morning feeling unusually lazy and relaxed. I had heard an Owl hooting in the night, but apart from that my night had been dark and quiet. I saw the solar plexus spinning. I thought how dizzy this could make me, but it slowed down, stopped spinning, and made the heart symbol; everything became very still. I remembered the meditation where there was ecstasy to be found both Above and Below, and I saw myself as the point in between. I saw the Sun Moon Dance Tree and I called to the Creator. My head centre opened and began to perceive the energy of creation, Breath, Matter, Movement: the generative matrix of our world in Joseph's teachings. This Life-energy came down as a Blue Light and it travelled into my heart centre. I saw the two halves of the heart centre and the blue ball of light came to rest high up on the centre line.

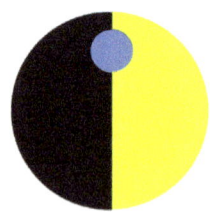

blue light in the heart

I came to meditate one morning, as I did every morning at this time, immediately I saw three Eagle feathers. This time the feathers were tied to a spear. I concentrated on them and one feather, a black feather with a white spine, took my attention and, from my viewpoint, hung, pointing downwards, on the right of the spear shaft. The space to the right opened up and a Being came in. I said some prayers to this presence, prayers that perhaps I don't remember now, about remaining open and being with my intent pure.

Then a much larger black feather appeared also pointing downwards towards the root centre. In the root centre I chanted: "wahohm, wahohm, wahohm, wahohm," the sound of water on Joseph's teaching tape. Chanting, I moved up the energy centres from the bottom to the top, visualizing them as I moved. When I got to the heart centre, a white feather appeared pointing upwards and with it came Alexander and Joseph and the Being Beyond, like echoes of one another.

3 feathers on a spear

I looked at the root and heart centres; they reminded me of a spirit level, and I used them to check the horizontal and vertical alignments of my body.

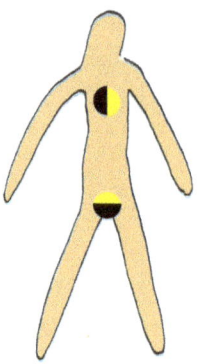

spirit levels

I seemed to hear a Spirit call me and say: "Stay in the colour Blue." I went to the circle of Blue Light in my heart centre and I rested there. I felt very great changes in my body, a conscious loss of my normal body and an expanding awareness of my spirit body. I felt an opening up of my right-hand side which caused a great shift, and I found that I was becoming a bird; much to my joy it was the white-faced Eagle with the brown body from the skin covered shelter of the Ancestors.

Filled with happiness, I flew up from the circle of the Sun Moon Dance arbour and glided above it. Viewed from above the arbour is rimmed with blue because of the blue waterproof sheeting that shades and shields the dancers in their rest places. I felt extremely happy that, in the joy of taking flight, I had indeed stayed where the Spirit asked me in the colour Blue, and that by flying I had discovered the dance arbour in my heart. Within the blue circle, was the medicine Tree, golden-yellow in the Black Light of the visionary world, and I knew that the Yellow Light is in the centre of the Tree, and that my Teachers are there.

in the blue

The Fisher

One morning I lay down to meditate and immediately I was aware of the very top left-hand side of my spirit body. I saw that this area was wide open. I concentrated on this and waited. A hot sweat came in from there and went down my body into my toes, making me aware of every part of myself. I stayed with the non-knowing of this sensation for as long as I could, following the movement of the in-coming as it moved through me. Eventually, I saw a Spirit with long braided hair.

I looked and looked at this figure and felt it enter into me. I felt myself take on many of the aspects and much knowledge from this Being. I allowed that to happen: "Be calm. Be still." I heard the name 'Black Eagle'. Recalling how I messed up the experience with my opinions when I had heard that name before, I thought as little as I could. I heard myself call him: "Father." I guessed he was a man of wisdom, a Grandfather, but the word 'Father' came, more easy to say, and every Grandfather is a Father too. During this prolonged contact, the image of a volcanic crater appeared with the instruction: "Wait, wait, wait." And strangely it was possible to wait by looking into the molten-red heaving mass of magma in the crater of this volcano which, impossible as it seems, enables me to be calm and still.

My energy centres opened, slowly, slowly, slowly, down, down, down, with the most important moment being the opening of the root centre where the Void became apparent. Suddenly this became a journey when prior to that it had been receptive feeling. I stood on the edge of the precipice and I knew that I was going to jump. I stretched my arms out and dived into the black abyss.

I was falling in the Void and I wondered what would happen. Far above me, I saw the image of the Being I will call 'Black Eagle' who keeps reminding me that the tops of his braids have red cloth tied around them. I saw him sitting on the lip of the Void and, as if it was a great lake, I saw that he had a fishing rod. The line was dangling down into the Void and I was the bait on the hook. Yes, I was the earthworm on the hook, and all the potential possibilities of form, which are floating in the Void, would swim towards me as a great attraction and, in that way, some of them would get hooked and pulled out. I got the feeling that this was a way to change the present status of our world.

But that feeling was miles away from the visual imagery of the Fisher of the Void, and, hanging on the hook, I was most interested to see what strange Beings would come up from the depths attracted by this bait. It was like watching a film taken very deep in the Ocean and glimpsing the creatures which turn up there; creatures that have never been seen before. That is what it reminded me of. There was no colour there, just the blackness and whitish silver outlines like skeletal beginnings of forms. There was no fear in this journey; the image of the earthworm that the Eagle ate had returned and it brought many things into focus, I was hooked and happy.

I was brought back a way, and a white figure 8 was laid out on a white visionary field. The Spirit, 'Black Eagle', came with colours, and I had a clear vision of a circular blue lake on the right and a red volcanic crater on the left filling the spaces of the number 8.

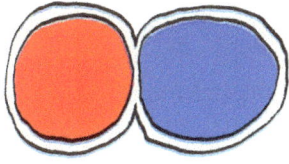

crater and lake

Around and between them was a white wall; it was very thin, and the thought was: "Imagine what would happen if the crater and the lake joined." There would be a most incredible explosion. The colour White was the barrier that held these two colours apart, thank goodness.

At the Red Rock

When I came to meditate ...... I have to think how the journey started now because, when I go through what happened, I keep going off into new experiences, but .... I suddenly became aware of the ceremony of cutting down the Tree that was to be planted in the centre of the arbour for the Sun Moon Dance. I became focused on the part of the Tree below the cut. Unaccountably, this part of the Tree, pale yellow at the Dance, was now pitch black and suddenly the Grandfathers arrived; the Ancient Grandfather on my left and the Grandfather of the Volcano, the younger one, the one I called 'Father', on my right.

They took me and spread-eagled me over the Void. My solar plexus opened and the energy from the Void rushed in. I took this energy and suddenly, in among the blackness, I saw a red boulder. It did not look very big, but, as the Grandfathers rushed me towards it, it became bigger. They placed me under this boulder. The boulder balanced gently above me, just one small part of it touching my solar plexus; it continued to expand and became as large as the world, but still it was just a lump of red rock.

I became most aware of the Ancient Grandfather, with his loving presence came his greyness and his gentle yellow colour. I spoke to him: "Grandfather, help me! Grandfather, whose bones are my bones, help me!" Help is the colour Yellow of this Grandfather and, when I was completely helped, I saw the head and the eye of the Eagle. The Eagle enfolded me into its body, and I heard that I was accepted by the Eagle and I understood that the acceptance came at the Sun Moon Dance: when I danced the Eagle, I finished a process.

The next time I came to meditate, the Ancient Grandfather returned. He was sitting astride a horse and I had my arm resting upon the horse's shoulder. Soon I found myself within the horse. The Grandfather said to me: "Nothing else can come into the place where you are. Find out what you are. Find out what is yours." I observed the dark space inside the horse, and I knew that with a very simple mental effort on my part it was the case that nothing else could come in. I waited and checked myself and waited. Eventually I saw an Eagle standing on the ground, a black Eagle with a white face. I looked harder at it; I saw a Vulture. Then I saw the shining round top of a single mushroom growing in the space. I saw a blue sphere of energy with hints of purple on its edges. Strange as this set of seeings was, they were somehow mine.

Late in the year my Teacher and I travelled to Australia. We travelled there to attend the first Sun Moon Dance in the southern hemisphere, a dance that Joseph would Chief, and to attend the Sound Chamber Conference being held the following weekend.

The day before leaving, my early morning meditation started with my seeing great ranks of spirits in front of me and understanding that these were all spirits who wished to help in the work at hand. There were ranks upon ranks of them. I looked and looked, turning my head to the left and to the right to try to see them all, and then bringing my attention back to the centre. I addressed all those ranks of spirits: "Yes, it is me. I need all the help I can get from everyone who is interested in this project because I have forgotten everything, and I don't know what I am doing."

Then I felt overwhelmed by the thousands of spirits who were there. How would I cope if they all stepped forward to help me? Something told me this was a pretty stupid thought, which related only to the human world. I also imagined that there must be some spirits in the multitude who were not well motivated, and this again was pointed out to be a silly thought. The Spirit I call 'Black Eagle' stepped forward from the crowd and he looked different; he looked like half the wing of a bird.

The next day, my Teacher and I travelled to Australia. After the Sun Moon Dance and the Conference, we got a lift to Melbourne and hired a car to drive to Ayers Rock. On the third day of our travelling, we began to see many flying Eagles, then we came across a dead one on the verge. We pulled the car over; I got out, ran back and crouched down beside it. I had never been so close to an Eagle and I looked at it intently, touching the wings, the legs and the feet, and feeling the lethal sharpness of the talons. Within less than a kilometre of this one there were two more. One, a very large bird, was completely dismembered; its liver, separated from its body, was lying in the centre of the road. I carried the remains of this Eagle off the road and picked up some of the scattered feathers that were blowing in the wind.

We travelled on. At the time I didn't feel that there was anything spiritually significant about this experience. It was more of a desperate tragedy to me than anything else; they came down to eat the road kills and, gorged, were too heavy to take off again becoming road kills themselves. But I did recall that the Eagle which I connected to at the seminar was a dead Eagle with a white face, beak and feet, and I noticed that these dead Eagles, Wedge-tailed Eagles, called 'Bungil' by the original people, have white faces, white beaks and white feet; their plumage is in many shades of brown and their flight feathers are black.

My Teacher was very keen to go to the Red Centre and he was also sure that something amazing would happen there. On our journey he had told me that Uluru, the original name of the Rock, was like the Holy Grail. I was prepared to go along with that, but consciously I didn't have a great impulse to go there; dancing in the Sun Moon Dance and meeting Joseph were my reasons for being in Australia.

It took three and a half days driving to reach the National Park. There wasn't a room to be had at the resort. We were fortunate that we had tents, and we got pitches on the campsite. We arrived in the early evening and, having put up our tents, we drove to the sunset viewing point and watched the Sun set on the greatest Rock on Earth. We watched with the many other people who were doing the same thing. It was a truly amazing spectacle. As the changing light cast different shadows on the Rock I saw a great hunched woman, I saw a totem bird on a stick, and I saw two serpent heads looking out towards us; look as I might, I could never see those serpent heads again. After the sunset viewing, we drove further into the Park in the dusk. It was our luck that other people went back to their hotels to eat and so the Park was deserted at this time of day. After a few minutes we were at the base of Uluru, we parked the car and went to touch the mighty Red Rock.

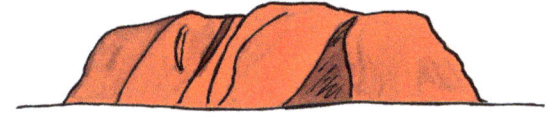

Uluru

The next evening as the Sun set, we drove again into the park and decided to walk the Mutitjulu path and, as darkness gathered around us, we walked into the long gulley. My Teacher was leading the way; he suddenly stopped, seeing ahead the deep dark drop of the Void. It was the black surface of a water hole. In the darkness we stood at the edge of the pool of the Void, we sang and played clap sticks. The shining quarter Moon was directly above us and, as we looked up at it, the dark shape of a large bird flew over.

During the night after this walk, to my surprise, Eagle spirits came to visit me and, as they circled around, I felt the touch of their wings. This helped me to find all the hidden levels of what had happened the day I carried the dead Eagle off the road. I realized that my connection to the Eagle in this world had been firmly established on that day and that the Wedge-tailed Eagle, lanky and ragged-looking, Vulture-like in its habits, was the Eagle which energised me. By that I mean that through the bodies of that Eagle species, my physical Being became acquainted with the vibration of Eagle-ness in the world of every day.

The first thing we did the next day was to walk the Mutitjulu path in daylight. It was extremely interesting to compare the two experiences. In the daylight it was a beautiful place, full of dragonflies, some vibrant red, others electric blue, very different to the echoing dark Void of the night before.

That evening we explored the Mala walk. I didn't imagine it could be better than the other track! I felt we passed through death by the cave of the 'Itjaritjari', the elusive marsupial mole, and then we found the cavernous overhang where four Beings are present.

4 rock beings

Although this wave cave is formed by wind erosion, the overhang is like a petrified ocean wave and the outlines of fossilised shells are still visible in the roof from the time when, millions of years ago, the red desert was a tropical sea. One of the four Rock Beings connected strongly with me as we sang and played the clap sticks there; the music we made was magical and opened up the spiritual space so amazingly that I felt a great excitement.

Leaving the wave cave, we seemed to pass through a gateway. I felt rather nervous and looked round as if something was following us and my Teacher, feeling it too, turned and smiled at me. I thought that was the end of the experience but no such thing, around the next corner we passed the cave that is sacred to women. There was such a fearsome guardian in the rock in front of that cave that I averted my eyes as I did not dare look in. We walked on into another gulley; the Moon was shining bright above it. Deep in the gulley the path came to an abrupt end. I stood there looking up at the sheer cliff face; the tremendous force of lifting upwards, up the cliff and out into the Universe, was just staggering and I felt myself flying up the vertical face; I was off. Suddenly the face of Joseph was in front of me as if to stop me flying away completely and that experience ended. When it was time to go, I was too awe-struck to turn around and walk back along the track, so, leaving with proper reverence, I backed out of that place.

That night I had a very confusing time where I was gripped tight in my solar plexus. I saw a giant aboriginal woman. Then suddenly the Eagle was standing beside me in such a realistic manner that I was completely shocked. At one point I opened my eyes, I had gone to bed with my tent flap open so that I could see the stars, and with a great swoosh a group of ancestral spirits took me to the stars. At another time I was lying on my back and my arms, which were for some reason bent and pointing upwards, shook violently. I was detached from this; it was as if my body was a rag that some spirit force was shaking, and I just witnessed it. My solar plexus was indeed twisted and shaken for much of the night. Those were our experiences at the Red Rock and the next day we left for Melbourne and our flight home.

I-ii

awareness of self

Houses to Live in

I found myself standing high up on the edge of a snow-covered mountain ridge. I wondered what I was doing up there. Looking down I could see far below a bright green valley with a group of pretty little houses clustered together; it looked a bit like Switzerland. I thought: "Do I want to go down into the valley, to the village, to the people?" I looked around for the downward path. There was no path. I recognized that my human impulse was to leave the mountain and go down to the warmth and safety of the village, but the fact there was no path puzzled me: "How did I get here?"

The Eagle presence came to me, and I saw that the Eagle was tearing at the body of a dead man and eating his flesh. I was shocked; was this a climber who had fallen? I saw there were some documents dropping out of his coat pocket and I picked them up. They looked official, printed on white paper in heavy black type.

I saw the word 'Lister'. Maybe he was Mr Lister, or was Lister his christian name? Then there was a bigger document, which I did try to scan, it seemed to be some kind of travel permit. Yes, lots of confusing thoughts went through my head. like: "What will they think when they find this body ripped up and eaten by the Eagle?" But: "Will they ever find this body because it has been ripped up and eaten by the Eagle?" It was quite shocking to me that the Eagle was eating human flesh. I also realized: "The Eagle has no desire to fly down into the valley and I am with the Eagle."

Turning its back on the valley, the Eagle took off, flying very low. I travelled with the Eagle. The snow was rose pink and the sky was pale blue. We passed over a white hare sitting among the snow mounds. The Eagle wasn't hungry, having eaten its fill, and it greeted the Snow Hare. I was pleased that the Eagle did not need to eat this carefree animal because it was eating men (better say 'humans' here, don't want to offend anybody).

With the occasional wing-flap, we glided on, eventually we landed on a rock and I perceived the Great Spirit, because that is what the Eagle had done, it had brought me close. I have lost what happened there.

I came back, feeling ready to carry on with my journey in this world. I thought: "The Eagle was eating a Lister." It came to me that the Lister is the person who listens. I knew that the Eagle had finished consuming Lister and that I was the next person that the Eagle would eat.

Keen to work more often with my Teacher, I conceived the notion to buy a house near the place where he lived and often taught, as this was a seven-hour drive from where I lived and worked. I began to look for such a property, and soon I found a small red painted wooden shack in a very run-down condition that had been on the market for years. It was called Drum View, a name which appealed to me vastly.

Drum View

I just need to think about the beginning of the meditation. I found myself connecting to the forest around Drum View. I saw the many mice living in the house and thought about the humane trap I might use to catch them. I found myself inside the house renovating it. A shadow came into my mind; it was a Wolf, ethereal, causing things to happen.

The Wolf came, right through the walls, into the house and began to push me into one of the corners. With its snout it pushed me right through the point of the corner where the walls meet the floor, that point where three planes meet. I went through that point and came into another world. There was a radical change in my consciousness, and I thought: "This is where I can begin to travel." But I didn't travel. I stayed very still in this place of altered awareness and waited.

Soon there was an arrival; it was the Eagle. The Eagle took me and flew. We landed at a strangely suburban address: 4 Long Hassle, Evergreen Road. I was so surprised to land at such a, well, ordinary house, if you like, that I decided to try to remember the address and the surrounding location.

Encountering the Power

Although our relationship is on the rocks, my morning meditation practice began with the overwhelming presence of the sweet, gentle side of my partner. I didn't want it, I wanted to pass through it, I didn't want to become ensnared in it because, although it was not evident at that moment, I knew that there was a trap of suffering in there and it couldn't be any other way.

I went through this atmosphere out onto the Great Plains. I felt sure I could get to the Ancient Grandfather who lovingly helps me. I moved through my body from right to left, looking, looking, looking for the Grandfather. Eventually I saw him sitting on his horse. I jumped up onto the back of the grey horse behind him and leaned my body against his. The grey mare's mane and our hair streamed out in the wind that was blowing cold upon our backs. Hunching up, we bent even farther forwards. I felt it might rain.

From the Grandfather's back, the colour Black flowed into me, and everything became pitch black. I travelled in the blackness and I found the colour Blue. I concentrated on that. After a while the colour Red became visible. I concentrated on the Red. The two colours were extraordinarily beautiful, purely there against the blackness of the Void. Perhaps by mixing, but that wasn't clear, the colour Purple filled the space until it was the only colour visible. I stayed with the Purple for a long time, and the teaching Joseph gave me in Australia: "Become the Power" came to me. I allowed things to become.

The Eagle came in the Purple Light and with the Eagle came Drum View. I am regretting not bidding more for this quaint building as someone else turned up with an offer and it has gone to their higher bid. The Eagle rolled the image of Drum View up into a tiny red ball and placed it in the left-hand side of my body, just above the hip joint, where it became no more than a flake of red paint. The Eagle said: "Scrape that flake of paint away." The paint scraping fell. I was crying: "No! no!" as I watched it descend into the vast ocean of the Void. The flake of paint fell, down, down, down through the stellar waters and landed on the bottom among all the other bits and pieces that had been cast away. The image of the Grandfather came back to me and the words 'Vacant Possession' rattled in the wind blowing through my empty head. I thought about the nature of the self and asked myself a few questions about what was going on. Well, let it be called 'Vacant Possession', that's fine by me; I am just a wrecked old building.

Before I began meditating this morning, my navel centre was aching, aching, aching. The aching had begun the night before after playing the drum and trying to be open to experiences beyond my understanding. I have really come to the firm conclusion now that the pain is caused by resistance in parts of myself, so I lay with the intent to release the pain, and my navel centre slowly relaxed more and more. When the pain was gone, I concentrated on becoming the Power. The Power was there; it was a feeling that moved through my bodies and made them aware. The Power moved for a long time, whatever a long time is in the meditative state.

Eventually I began to sense the immanent arrival of the Eagle. I encouraged the image of the Eagle, focusing on it by thinking of my contact with the australian Wedge-tailed Eagles. When the Eagle-ness was strongly present, I rested there. I prayed to the Eagle which had become in me and I said: "Stay with me. Be in me." Nevertheless, at times unpleasant things, particularly emotional things, would emerge, like an unpleasant situation from years ago would suddenly strike me and cause a disruption in the beautiful peace of the Power. When this happened, I searched for the good aspects of that experience and I recalled the instruction the Ancient Grandfather once gave to me: "Learn to love what you hate." An instruction that had caused me then to burst out crying: "How can I love someone's mean and selfish intent?" In my reflection now, I discovered that it is possible to hate bad intent and also to love the Spirit of the person who carries it in their life, and I decided: "I will work to resolve and go beyond these pains because they affect my ability to be open to new experiences."

I asked the Eagle to stay with me and I saw bird droppings splattered on a rock. I didn't want to see that. Then I thought ironically: "That is probably the only way the Eagle can express me." So, I looked again at the stained rock and next to it I saw the gigantic leg and foot of the mighty Eagle Spirit. That filled me with joy, but at the same time the image of the legs and feet of the road-killed Wedge-tailed Eagle came into my mind, and the leg and foot of the Spirit Eagle became the rotting legs of that Eagle and I knew for sure that my contribution to the Spirit of the Eagle would always be subject to decay, to change, to transformation.

The experience I am going to record now will sound like a dream, but it was beyond the realm of dreaming because of my state of consciousness. However, although fully aware, I was not in the place where I was, lying on my back meditating at 7 a.m. in my North Yorkshire house. Instead, I was in my bed in the house where I was born, in Suffolk.

I was waking up from deep sleep and it was dark. I put my hand over the side of the bed, and I found two Eagle wings there, black in the blackness. I picked them up and, laying them upon my chest, I entered an extremely altered state of consciousness where spirits came into me and began to move my spirit body. They pulled me out of my body and hung me in the air above the bed, upside down, suspended by my left leg. As I was pulled out of my body and hung in this fashion, I hoped to goodness that nobody would come and see me hanging there, but I knew the space was completely safe and that the spirits would not have done this if there was a chance of anybody witnessing it. So, I hung upside down above the bed suspended by the spirit power.

As I hung upside down there, experiencing the very peculiar sensations in my body that go with that type of experience and feeling completely safe in the hands of the spirits, one took hold of my left ankle and began to pull my leg again. I felt again a surge of adrenaline and I decided to go with it. I wondered what I would experience as I was pulled out of this second body. I had the belief that I would suddenly start to see things in a different way and that would be incredibly exciting, but then this thought came to me: "I am on my own, without a travelling companion." And just by the very act of thinking that thought I seemed to stop the process.

The spirits stopped pulling me, but I was still hanging upside down. I stayed very still, waiting, not moving any part of me, mental, physical, spiritual, or emotional, but eventually, after a long time of nothing happening, I did move and I was lying here where I was, but I didn't notice any change at all from one state to another, which deeply puzzles me.

I believe in the reality of this experience. I was completely sure that I was conscious and that it was actually happening. The feelings in my body and in my mental state were of a particular kind that I rarely do experience, and I thank the spirit powers for these experiences, which feel to me like food.

The Eagle's Body

Still travelling up and down the country to work with my Teacher and, also, run my business, I attended another seminar. About the third day we took a journey to the lower world and I need to say something about the instructions for the journey: we should go to a beautiful place in nature, call the power animal and exchange gifts there. Then we would journey with this animal to find something that we had lost in our childhood, and we could have this given back to us. We should put the lost thing into our body and come back. That is how the instructions were given.

As soon the rapid opening drumbeats started, I saw the colours green and gold. I thought: "I do know a beautiful place in nature that has these two colours, but where is it?" I found myself descending into the arbour of the Sun Moon Dance ceremony where the radiating golden tracks made by the dancers' feet contrast with the green grass spaces between them. I was standing looking at the Dance Tree. A bird landed on the top of the Tree. I wondered: "Is it an Eagle?" I felt awed by this possibility, but it seemed rather smaller than an Eagle. I called it down. It flew down onto my right wrist. It was a white Blackbird with a yellow beak.

The drumming changed to a steady beat marking the beginning of the journey. The white Blackbird flew violently at my right eye and tore it out with its beak. I was completely shocked. I thought: "Oh-aaah, what's going on? I want my eye back." It seemed unlikely that I would get it. I demanded it; there was no response. Then I said to the bird: "Well, you can have that eye as a gift." Immediately the bird flew away with my eye and I was left thinking: "But that was the Being I was going to exchange gifts with, and it has just flown off with my eye."

I turned to look at the Dance Tree again; it was the most enormous White Eagle. All around me, the white feathers were close. I wasn't standing on the ground looking up; I was standing in the eye socket of the Eagle. The right eye was missing, and the inner recesses of the eye socket were brown. Again, totally shocked by this situation, I wondered what to do and I thought: "This eye socket is actually somewhat like a cave, and we are supposed to be journeying into the lower world, so I will walk in." I walked in; it was the entrance to an underworld. I stood there and I worried: "But I haven't got an animal to travel with me." The deep voice of the Eagle spoke to me and said: "As long as you are within my body you are travelling with me, so, travel without fear."

The spinal column was a golden ladder and I began to descend. I climbed down, down, down into the body. Soon I found myself looking horizontally into the liver. I entered the liver. Integrated now into the Eagle's body, I began to feel the journey taking place in my own body. I entered the gall bladder and words came to me: 'the bitter sea'. A black boat was stationed by the shore and an immense, flat, motionless expanse of dark Ocean stretched away. I stepped into the black boat and it began to move out across the inky water.

I noticed a tall black bird standing ahead of me at the prow. Its wings were so tightly folded against its body that it looked as if it never used them. I wondered why a bird would be a ferryman of the underworld. I called it to me. It came to my left wrist and I said: "Look, I can see by your yellow legs and feet that you are a hunting bird. You are a Hawk. Go, fly for me, and bring me a present." The bird flew away and I was left alone in the boat. I asked myself: "Was that a good idea? Did I just send the power animal away? Am I afraid?" But I remembered the words of the Eagle. I was within the Eagle therefore I was not afraid.

The boat moved on across the black waters; it had no sails, no oars, no motor, no rudder, no crew, and yet it travelled purposefully over the calm and barren waste of the bitter sea. Suddenly, without warning, it spun round, one and a half turns, and I found myself in a different world. This world was very thin horizontally; there was only a narrow gap between the floor and the ceiling. There were some energies here that were like silk, that is the nearest I can describe them. They crackled and they felt like silk, they moved in long formations made of many fibres, which made them seem to be like silk scarves. Some were silver and some were gold. They entered my body through my navel centre, spiralling down as if they were being pulled by a whirlpool, slowly coiling themselves up as they entered into my body in that way.

Once inside me, the scarves began to stretch themselves throughout my body and make me aware of all my body. The fibres ran down my legs, they ran in my arms, they ran everywhere, and I began to get a different sense of my body which was not a thing composed of arms and legs; it was a thing composed of hundreds and thousands upon thousands of these filaments.

It became apparent to me that the thing I had lost was the knowledge of the nature of my body. As I grew older, this is what had disappeared, or been taken away from me, or I had no longer been able to connect to. I lay now in this horizontal layer of existence and began to stretch the fibres with my will, began to go even further into every nook and cranny. I was reminded of coral, when the polyps with all those little hairs come out and flick around in the water and can be withdrawn and disappear again into the hard, coral case. I ran my fibres everywhere in this horizontal world and became aware of everything and knew that I could know everything that was there. Everything that was there was composed of light of various colours, green and pink and blue and gold. Everything was transparent in form and the fibres of my Being could touch everything.

At this point I paused, and I returned to the beginning of the journey and travelled it again, more intensely. I didn't ask myself why the bird took my eye. I didn't ask myself whether the socket of the Eagle's eye was a cave. I didn't have to try to discover at what place I had arrived, and so everything happened more intensely and with more impact on my body. I came back to the same place. I wondered what would happen next.

I began to look at the fact that this world which I was in was not very deep but extended vastly horizontally. I looked up and above I could see that the bitter sea was above this world and above that were all the other layers of my Being. I drew all the filaments back from the horizontal world and gathered them into my navel centre. Then, in one movement, I pushed them out. As they shot up vertically through the layers of my Being, they disconnected all the connections which held that Being together as something real: it did not fragment but the restricting cohesion was lost. The bunch of fibres, which left my navel centre packed close together, spread out as they rose higher, spread out into what was like a Tree made of vertical shooting fibres of light.

I was looking at this Tree when the black bird landed high up in the branches. I called out: "Come down. What have you brought me?" It had brought me a silver ring with a design engraved upon it. I put the ring on the third finger of my right hand. I was looking at it, trying to work out what the design might be when I began to get annoyed with the bird. I don't know for what reason, but it had gone back to its original non-flying form. I took hold of it with my left hand. I felt how the hard feathers on its wings were compacted and how they seemed to be stuck to its body. I pushed it into my body, to the right of my heart, immediately everything felt extremely bad. I didn't like to have this strangely static bird inside me, and I didn't like the ring. I pulled the bird out and threw it away. I took off the ring and I threw the ring away.

I looked again at my great luminous Tree body and I wondered what to do with it. I opened it out so that there was a big space in the centre of all the fibres, thinking: "I could make something in here that makes things. That would be interesting." But I didn't do it.

Then a vision of the Eagle's face came to me, one of the eyes was missing. I said to myself: "I can make the eye of the Eagle. I can give the Eagle back its eye." Maybe it took all the fibres that I had, or maybe I got so absorbed in the task that I put all of myself into it. The eye of the Eagle was back in the socket and perfect. I was just beginning to think that, as I was now an eye, I could look out and see what the Eagle saw, when the drumming changed. The journey was over.

The journey was a very absorbing and pleasant experience. I feel that the gift I received was the return of my body awareness. And the gift that I gave? Reluctantly I gave my eye to the small and spiteful bird at the beginning of the journey, and at the end I gave myself, my eye, to the Great Bird who protected me and let me travel within it. Thank you, Eagle.

Back at home, about a month later, I came to meditate in the morning, and I saw a silver mirror lying in the navel centre, like a little puddle of mercury in my belly button. I looked hard at it and a voice said to me: "Learn the lesson of the silver light." Or maybe it said: "Learn the mystery of the silver light." Or maybe it said: "Learn the power of the Silver Light." Or maybe it said one sentence that meant all these things.

The silver mirror condensed into a sphere and, flying through space, arrived by the Mutitjulu pool at Uluru. I arrived with it. I was standing there when the feathered legs of the road-killed Eagle became visible to me; those putrefying legs were a deep contrast to the red purity of Uluru and the silver surface of the Mutitjulu pool, but they were the thing that caught my attention. I began to pick up all the dismembered Eagles from the road where we had found them and, as I picked them up, I rubbed the bloody smashed bits of the Eagles onto my body and I felt the blood and the deadness enter me. I took the big Eagle's liver from the middle of the road and put it into my body.

Then the Eagle began to tear at me. It tore out my third eye, my centre of seeing, and I thought: "Will I see more now the Eagle has pulled out this eye?" I looked and I saw light. I wondered: "Is this seeing more, or less?" It pulled out my throat centre, and the space there got bigger. It tore out my heart centre, where an open blue sky in a crystal-clear world was apparent. Turning around in my heart centre, so that its head was now facing towards my feet, it tore at my solar plexus, and pure Green Light, appeared in that place.

Then I became aware that another Being was standing in front of me. Solar plexus energy travelled out from each of us towards the other. Floating out of my solar plexus, I saw a bowl made of stainless steel which, due to its weight, dropped down between us, farther and farther and farther, like it was falling into infinity. Down, down, down, down it fell until it landed at our feet. It was a tiny silver speck down there and, in that way, I realized how big we were. Meanwhile the energy between our solar plexus centres had met and merged and I became more aware of this other Being which had, at that point, the vague form of a human but no colour and no distinguishing features.

I felt a change and before me was an open Hand. The solar plexus of the Being was now the centre of the palm of this Hand and my solar plexus was holding itself against it. I raised up my arms and stretched my out legs so that I made an X-shape, I hooked myself onto the top of the palm with my fingers and to the bottom of the palm with my toes and the Power was coming through the centre of this Hand into me. The fingers of the Hand shut over me and opened again; a great breath blew upon me:

"Whhhhhhuuuuuuuu-aaaaaahhhhhh"

and blew me away like a piece of crumpled paper. Soon as I could I was back there again, and that Great Hand brought the other Great Hand behind me and .... I have got a blank moment ... um....... as the second Hand closed over my back, I felt Power come into the back of me as well as into the front. I was held between them, as if the Hands were in an attitude of prayer with me in the middle. Then there was a long period where I simply tried to come into line with, or integrate, or become one, with this Power. Voices were encouraging me to, you know, let go, ... open up this, ... do that, ... do the other. And I did. I want to go there again. I feel deeply, um, miffed that I had to return because of Time. I will try to enter that place again, if I can manage it.

A House to Live in

I began this journey aware of the spirits; aware that they were here, that I was connected, and that we were longing to communicate with each other. I went back to the walk I took last night across the upland Fell. In the evening light, I had lain on my belly on the smooth rock at the head of a dry waterfall that I often visit. Although I knew, from experience, this was a place of great peace, relaxation, and healing, for some reason I was restless, and I couldn't stay there; I felt impelled to make a trip to the cave in the gulley. As I walked, I was wondering if moving from the previous spot had been the right or the wrong thing to do. How easy it would have been to lie on that warm rock and receive those pulses in my navel centre, absorb the sunlight and be absent.

So, in my meditative journey, I was asking myself again if I was foolish to always push myself to the limits when I found myself within the cave. Last night I had only glimpsed the interior as I scrambled up the rocks towards the entrance. The climb was gritty and slippery; my physical body did not like it at all. The rocks and mud had a strong earthy clay smell; a smell I wasn't sure I liked. I sniffed it a lot, asking myself: "What's wrong with it?" and the answer was: "Nothing." It was just the natural odour and inconvenience of the muddy wetness of the terrain that was off-putting to me as a modern human Being.

Now I lay in the cave in my meditation. I said quietly: "Mother, Mother," and I connected deeply to the dark Mother of Lost Beginnings, to the ancientness of our Mother the Earth. Looking around I caught a glimpse of a frantic creature, a shocking sight, a black horse in a state of pure wildness and terror, flaring nostrils foaming white in the gloom. I asked myself: "Do I want to travel with THAT?" I certainly did not, but I felt that if I lost this opportunity in this place of lost beginnings, I might not get another chance, so I searched and found that wildly crazy horse again. The tensed body was glistening and sharp, like obsidian, and I felt I might be cut to ribbons. We travelled on a rapid and volatile journey; the horse rolled into a ball and flew through the great lost spaces, bringing me to the Edge where everything changes into something else and stopping dead at that point. I hurtled on and, catching a momentary glimpse of the thin line which joins the one place to the other, I went rolling into the other place.

In the space where the horse had thrown me, I saw a small black Rock. I went to it and, enfolding it in my body, I entered in. As I entered, I became aware of Blue Light. It surprised me that the Blue Light, which I consider to be part of my origin, was accessible within this rock. I observed that the black was the atomic structure of the matter that defined the rock and the Blue Light filled all of the space between the atomic connections; the space within this small rock was endless, endless.

I was looking at it, feeling and thinking that there would be more to know, and that, maybe, I would entirely enter into the Blue through the web of the atomic structure of matter, when there was a blank patch and I found myself in the presence of the Great Spirit: that Great Spirit, so huge and far away, and yet so near and so easy to communicate with when I reach the place of communication. I spoke to the Great Spirit. I seemed to be very aware of what I needed to know, and I said: "Great Spirit, I, I use the wrong words, help me to speak the right words." I saw that the place I was drawing the wrong words from was the right-hand side. I should go to the more unknown left side in order to find the right words.

I looked at the Great Spirit and a line of spheres were emanating from there towards me. They looked like ball bearings, but they weren't shining silver, they were grey. The peculiar thing was that the closer to the Great Spirit they were the bigger they were, and the closer they were to me the smaller they were. They were teachings which were coming to me and it was clear that there was no interrupting this line of teachings which were being sent out. When the spheres arrived at me, they entered my solar plexus and I learnt things. Yes, I felt I didn't need to worry, they were coming. All I needed to concentrate on was finding in my self the right place to have the experiences which were available.

I became aware that I was looking and looking into an area of my travelling body at the back of my head above my left shoulder. I reached out and picked up a claw. It was an Eagle's claw, one of the sharp talons I had touched as I knelt beside the Wedge-tailed Eagle's body. Revisiting that contact with the dead australian Eagle, I entered into a deep meeting with the Spirit Eagle; a meeting so deep that my feet became the Eagle's feet. I bent down and I touched the feathered legs of the Eagle, the ragged trousers. I stayed with the Eagle Spirit for as long as I possibly could.

I slipped and I found myself in the bathroom at Fair View, the bungalow I am bidding for now, looking at the window with its pane of frosted glass thinking to myself: "I don't want frosted glass. I must change it to clear glass so that I can see the mountains." I heard clearly: "The Eagle has brought you to this place." So, I feel it is necessary to have the courage to put onto the tape that I believe that I will buy this house. Oh, spirits don't let me be proved to be wrong; it will be a hard thing for me to take.

Today, only a month after putting in my offer, the buying of Fair View is supposed to be completed. As I lay here reviewing my life up to this point, the impression of this square bungalow came, out of the blue. I thought: "Yes, this house is coming as a result of everything that went before."

The meditation that followed started in a cleft filled with the colour Red; then I saw red and green floating together, not mixing into another colour, but existing together in a place. I always find this combination rather shocking because the two colours are such opposites, but I looked at it for a while. Then the colour Blue began to appear. I rose up. The colour Blue was showing me that the Red and the Green were below and that I was travelling in the sky. The wings of the Eagle brushed against me; I was flying with the Eagle. I determined that I would open my perception as far as I was able in order to understand more about the nature of the Eagle Spirit. A Spirit that is very incomprehensible to me and that came in the night at Uluru as wings touching my body. I felt myself enter into the consciousness of the Eagle. I looked up, trying to reach the limits of its body, travelling in my mind towards the boundary of its head, but I did not get there. I could see the huge vastness of the Eagle stretching above me, but whether I could ever travel to and touch the periphery of its awareness I, ... I doubt.

I gave up my search for boundaries, and explored the left side of my head, looking for the Eagle there. This is what I was doing, searching for the Eagle-feeling and, when I felt it, trying to see it.

Reconnecting, I travelled with the Eagle again, and I saw a large round hole ahead of us. I heard: "This is a hole in experience." I must have arrived first at the hole as I was waiting there when the Eagle, on a flight path aimed to go straight through the hole, grabbed at me with its talons as it passed, but, like a film that is rewound and replayed, this happened more than once. I clung to the edge of this hole-in-experience and it may have been the fourth time the Eagle passed me that, clutched in its talons, I actually went through.

Now I was quite scared, so I just shut my eyes and let the Eagle carry me. Opening them for a milli-second, I saw a vision of a Dinosaur, which made me think that we must have travelled way back into prehistory. We landed at the base of a tree. The body of this tree was like the trunk of a fat Palm tree and, looking up, I saw that it was a gigantic Cycad. I went inside and I had the perception that I had been present at the beginning of Trees. I travelled upwards in the trunk. It was a long journey. At the very top there was a golden cone and the fronds of the bracken-like branches sprouted out from just below it. From this vibrating cone, an endless rain of golden spores was fountaining out into the atmosphere. I got the impression that from this Tree came the diversity of life on land, as if it was the generating engine of all that followed.

Yesterday the buying of the bungalow was completed. The solicitor's office closed at five thirty in the afternoon and at five twenty-five they rang me to say it was done. My partner has decided that this signals the end of our relationship and so it looks as if I will be totally dismantling my present life in the West and moving North.

Fair View

I am quite exhausted from driving for seven hours yesterday between one life and another, and I woke up very tired from disturbing dreams. As I began to meditate, I felt the Eagle Spirit entering my throat centre and, circling high in the air above me, it called with its piercing cry: "Lister, Lister." Calling to me, and I travelled up to be with the Eagle.

Suddenly I realized I was hearing a sentence repeated, again and again: "Do not let sadness enter, do not let sadness enter." I was very surprised to hear this sentence because I didn't realize that there was sadness, about moving, entering my heart centre and causing pain. I asked myself: "Am I sad, really? There is no doubt that this is what I want, and what am I leaving that I will regret?" But still I knew it was going to be quite hard to do what the voice asked. The Eagle took hold of me with its beak and gave me a shake, nothing drastic.

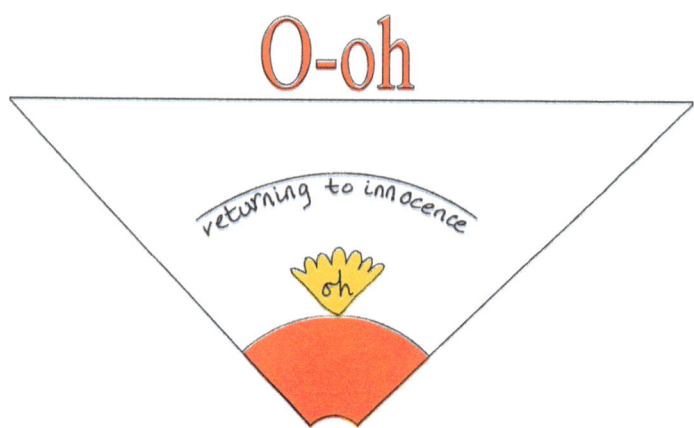

Being of Thunder

This morning I swiftly felt the power of the Wolf and, to my surprise, found myself travelling towards Drum View; a place I thought was finished with, but I was travelling towards the meeting with the Wolf there. The metaphoric nature of that experience was being clearly shown to me; it was a passing into the colour Red, into the North. As I passed through the walls of the house and came into my meeting with the Wolf, whose name is Loss, the scene translated itself to Fair View.

A perception opened in me and I saw that the Wolf power was surrounded by the Buffalo power. The Wolf power was grey and the Buffalo power around it was brown, forming a circle that supported the Wolf. The power of the Buffalo was nurturing, like the nature of the planet.

As this circle of awareness held my attention, I passed by the Sun Moon Dance Tree. The colour White entered the experience, and I knew that, through the power of the Sun Moon Dance, I was entering the whiteness of the Buffalo. I went into the White Buffalo consciousness, which was encircling my heart, and above it was the colour Purple, the colour of the consciousness of Joseph's spiritual input. The colour Green poured in through my lower centres, I was swept along in the greenness and my awareness of my spirit body increased dramatically.

During the times I have spent with my Teacher, on rare occasions, the clouds would gather and the sky would be filled with the rumblings of thunder, then he would talk about the Thunder Beings of New Mexico, and now I was able to see an image of a Thunder Being which took the form of a bird. The body of this Eagle-like Being was the shape of an equal-armed cross and the head was turned to one side. I was able to count a number of the larger feathers on the wings and tail. Along each forearm, there were four short feathers and there were three long flight feathers at the tip of each wing. In the tail, I counted seven feathers and the centre one was long, like one of the centre tail feathers of the Wedge-tailed Eagle, and that is when the image really came home to me. The two legs went out to the sides and the talons held what looked like round balls.

The next time I saw the Thunder Being, the experience began when the colours Black and Purple entered and took over everything. I felt myself going down, down, down, and because the direction was down into the Black Light accompanied by the light that I see with Joseph, I was quite happy to go down like that. When I reached the complete down-ness of the depths, the colour Green, which had swept me along on the last occasion, reappeared in the centre of these two colours, Purple and Black, and I was surprised.

I rose, but not of my own volition, the Green rose me, up, up, up, up, up, and, as I rose, I crossed a barrier into a golden-yellow place which was my heart centre. As soon as I arrived there, I felt the presence of other spirits who had once been people. What did

I hear? Something like: "Here, we are not separate." It was as if all the Lights who had walked the Earth were gathered in this golden-yellow centre. I enjoyed and was encompassed in that for a while.

Then my attention walked back to the centres below the recently crossed barrier and I appreciated that below the barrier I was, if I chose to be, separate and untouchable; everything that happened there was individual to me and had my own personal stamp, integrity and separation. I rose again into the golden-yellow place where I was immediately aware of the presence of the Thunder Being. I became more and more into the consciousness of that Being which formed as a vast yellow disc above, and below a black disc of a similarly vast size.

Then a voice said to me: "Learn to move." I thought the instruction was about moving to my new house; and in a way it was, but it was also about learning to move my travelling body. I tried to do this with my will, and I became exceedingly exhausted. The journey got hard, but I couldn't just leave. When I reach that particular state of consciousness, it becomes very agonizing and I am at the limit of endurance, but I can't drop out; the option is not there. It does not matter how screamingly tired I feel, I must continue, and so I did.

As the journey continued, the two discs of the Thunder Being both became yellow, yellow above and yellow below. Next I saw two similar discs, one on either side, on the joints of the wings, and these exactly corresponded to the pains in the ball joints of my shoulders that I have at present, which, when I look at them, are like golden balls of pain. Seeing the Eagle's energy discs there made me feel slightly better about these horrible pains. The final image of the Thunder Being was of another golden-yellow disc placed in the centre of Being, not in any of my energy centres but in the body of the Great Being in the realm where we are not separated.

Thunder Eagle

On the Sunday before the second Sun Moon Dance in England, I had my alarm set for 6 a.m. but I did not wake up. When I did eventually wake up, it was something like twenty to eight. What was I up to? I heard my partner get up. I thought: "I am not going to meditate today, what's going on?" I felt nothing, no spiritual connection, no incoming, nothing. I thought: "Well, I will just lie here for a minute or two."

And so, I lay there. Immediately, the spirits started talking to me. They said: "It is time that it does not matter what is happening around you, who is where and whether people are asleep. It is time NOW." I replied: "Oh! oh, ok." And they asked me what I was concentrating on now in my spiritual life? I saw the white trunk of the Sun Moon Dance Tree surrounded by blue above and green below, and the Tree came right into the centre of my Being. There were no barriers that separated me from the Tree vibrating there, and I gave this answer to the spiritual question: "I am allowing the colour White to possess me." And I thanked the colour White.

I began to think about the spirits who were talking to me and I asked: "Who are you?" The spirits replied: "Love." Standing in the whiteness, I realized: "I am light. I am light receiving help from love. Love and Light are in communication in me." To be standing in a place of light receiving love was a beautiful moment; I had found my placement and what did my placement mean? As I wondered, I found myself standing in the presence of the Giant Eagle; I was smaller than the size of one of its talons. Then, knowing that the Being was aware of me, I was awestruck. There was nothing for me to do in the presence of such Greatness except to acknowledge it and wait. And it kept me waiting. So, I did wait.

Then my mind slipped, and I thought of something else. At that moment the Eagle spoke to me and said gravely: "The two Grandfathers are here." They were. The Grandfather of the Volcano was on the left and the Ancient One was on the right. These Grandfathers became in me. They were right in the frontal lobes of my brain, so close and so equal that I could feel and see them both at the same time. The feelings were extraordinary, and normally, if I was not in the correct altered state, I would run from those feelings, but today I had no fear whatsoever and I was able to simply allow these feelings, these movements, these influxes of power, to enter my body and I felt better and better while this happened.

The Grandfathers' energies touched each other in the centre, but they did not overlap. They were working together in complete harmony. I was looking at the point where they met, in the very centre, and I asked them to send me a symbol to help me concentrate.

A very thin red ribbon was laid across my forehead and tightly tied round my head with a beautiful bow. A second one was tied across my heart, a third one across my solar plexus, and a fourth one across my navel centre. The Grandfather Spirits said to me: "As long as you are firing on four cylinders, everything will be right."

I felt those four energy centres activated and open and the Power was there. I thanked Joseph for his teaching about the Power because it has brought me to this point of deep connections with the spirits who love me, the spirits who love Love, the spirits who love world peace, and the spirits who love for people to reach their highest potential. Having four energy centres open and receiving the Power was, to me, a further understanding of the medicine wheel.

I had been very impatient to move to Scotland, now suddenly it came to me that maybe I need to do four Sun Moon Dances before I leave the West and go to live in the North. Whether that is the case or not, it has made me calm and it has made me stop getting in a sweat about the passing of time. I feel quite happy now that this move will take the time that it will take, and I am going to dance my third dance next weekend.

I danced in England, near Manchester.

After the dance, I felt very serene, very happy, and many challenges swiftly came to me from the world of every day. I woke up one morning very disturbed, very confused by the contradictions of anger, fear, desire and selfishness that had poured out of my partner the day before aimed at me. Sent to break up my calm, I think would be what I would say.

This attraction to have a go at me was not confined to my partner; it had started, away from home, only a few days after the dance. As I parked my car in the local town, a woman, who thought I had put a dent in the back of her car, ran up and attacked me verbally. I felt very relaxed as I knew I had not made the dent and I showed her that there was no protrusion and no mark on my car that matched up with the dent in hers. This seemed to enrage her even more and she demanded that I did not move until her husband returned. I happily stood there for about fifteen minutes while she sat, silent and hostile, in her car. When her husband returned, she showed him the dent and he said: "Oh, that has been there for ages." And I left. I was really puzzled: what was it about me that was causing such reactions? I concluded that my energy field was carrying the beauty of the Sun Moon Dance and that unhappy people could not bear to see it.

So that morning I lay horribly enmeshed in other people's anger and agony. Everything went black and, in the blackness, I saw Joseph. I called his name and I was surprised how easily the horrible confusion and battering I was experiencing disappeared, and a space was created in which I stood within Joseph's dark calmness. I have a tail feather of the Wedge-tailed Eagle that I would like to give to him, and that black feather came and laid itself upon me. Until I am able to give it to him, it would be there to help me.

Even though our relationship will soon come to an end, my partner's pain was hard to bear and in the afternoon of that day I gave him my dance. I was listening to him talking and, feeling his distress, I sent it to him energetically. I hope it made some difference for him. As for me, that giving taught me a lot about the transformational energy of the Dance. As I gave my dance away, I felt the energy leave me and it was devastating. Then I knew I must dance again and again so that one day I would come to a place where I would carry that energy all year, from one Dance to the next, and that would help to make it available to everyone.

In the evening, I felt that the spirits were very close, and it turned out that my partner wouldn't be back home until late. I ate and then I lay down, maybe just for a little while, to think about my life, and while I was doing this I suddenly felt the presence of Joseph arriving from a long way away and hard upon his heels came his brother, our Sun Moon Dance Chief in England. It was quite a surprise to me that they were both present but then I remembered that our Chief had said he would see Joseph in two weeks, and it was indeed a fortnight after the dance. I felt they were together, that they were talking, and that this is what had united us. I realized that the tail feather of the Wedge-tailed Eagle, which had come to help me earlier, had, without the physical feather yet leaving me, passed energetically from myself to my first Sun Moon Dance Chief, Joseph's brother, and from him to the first ever Sun Moon Dance Chief, Joseph Rael, Beautiful Painted Arrow.

Today is my birthday and as a birthday present, late last night, the spirits gave me a massive wedge of incomprehensibility. I saw a very strange and extraordinary Spirit. I could hardly comprehend its form, but I knew: "That is a Thunder Being." Composed of lines the form was black. There were wings and a centre circle of blackness that was something like a split link while above the shape was like the outline of an Eagle's head. It was a great present. This morning I have lain and constructed a picture of it in my mind, but last night this was not easy to do. I just had the awareness and a vague impression of it.

Prior to this, after being with my two Chiefs, my attention had wandered, but when this vision erupted, I became extremely interested and I believe this experience lasted for an hour or so. In fact, there were three Thunder Beings. If there were to be more than one, I was surprised that there weren't four, perhaps one for each cardinal direction, but no, I could only perceive three. In my mind now I see black and yellow, but last night I just saw three dark Beings. They took me into extremely altered places. I sang. I perceived my body in a whole new way.

I came back with a jolt that pulled my physical body upwards and spiralled my spirit body around, and I felt shocked when I got back and lay with a knot in my solar plexus for some time. Then I said to the spirits: "I am going to go away from this now and go to sleep." And that is exactly what I did.

I cannot imagine that I will get this journey down exactly right, but the spirits assured me, they assured me, when I was panicking as it got so complicated, that they would bring it to me again, again, and again until I got it. So, here is my attempt:

Yes, today I was free! There was clear space around me, and I entered the spirit lodge, a familiar place of safety. I went in highly aware, highly energised and, as soon as I was in that place, the colour Yellow began to spread from the centre, as it engulfed me and overwhelmed me the spirits asked me a question: "What is the colour Yellow?" I answered fairly quickly: "The colour Yellow is Be-ing. The colour Yellow is, um, everything that Be-es, everything that be-comes, everything that is."

Then the yellow was replaced with blue, and the spirits asked me very swiftly, very strongly, very abruptly: "What is the colour Blue?" I freaked out because I was still in the yellow and they were asking me a question that I felt I hardly knew the answer to. I knew I had to answer fast and not think too much about it. I said quickly: "The Blue is everything that flies in the sky and everything that swims in the sea. Please don't make me do this." But they did.

Then the colour Green came, and they said again: "And what is the colour Green?" I answered: "The Green is everything that grows. The Green is nourishment. The Green is how the spirit grows and develops and ....." I have lost it now! I just said: "The Green is everything that grows. It nourishes everything. It is how everything grows in Be-ing."

I was then ready to go on to the next colour, which was black, but the spirits shouted: "Stop! Stop. Stay still." I stood still in that place and into that place came purple light with emerald green. Those are the colours that I see with Joseph. Joseph came and I addressed a prayer to him: "Help me, Joseph, look, I am here, help me to learn. Oh, Beautiful Painted Arrow, please help me."

The arrow flew and embedded itself in my body. But, quite contrary to the Beautiful Painted Arrow that leaves the colours of the rainbow trailing behind it, this arrow was black. It had a triangle at the front end, a round stem, and at the back end, where the flight feathers would be, it had three horizontal bars. The longest was first on the shaft, then a shorter one, and then the shortest one at the end, with a small amount of the shaft pointing out behind that. The shaft was like a round wrought iron bar.

the arrow

The head of the arrow was embedded in my psyche, in the left-hand side of my body about the level of my belly button. There was no pain with this arrow.

I thought there were to be no consequences at all, but suddenly I was looking into the mouth of an enormous Snake and staring into the yellow tunnel of its throat. The jaws were closing round the lower part of my body and I felt the two fangs penetrate the soft part of my belly in the pelvic region; the fang that entered the left side of my body was blue and the fang that entered the right side was green. I wondered: "Am I going to suffer now and die?" Sensing the Ancient Grandfather, I said: "Grandfather, Grandfather, I am dying, I am dying. I ... am ... dying." And he agreed with me.

The red tongue of the Snake flickered, and the Grandfather pulled me backwards. I am getting a bit confused here, he pulled me backwards, and I think at this point the colour Black came. Yes, the colour Black, which I had expected earlier when the spirits told me to stop, came now. It poured into me and everything became black. I knew this was the Power, the Power that came through Joseph and was coming into me. He had said: "Become the Power." And so, I did that.

The beginning of the becoming was exciting, but then I didn't feel so brilliant and a little voice inside me said: "But I don't feel powerful." I had to laugh as I realized: "Oh, you thought that becoming the Power meant that you would be powerful, did you? Well, apparently that is not the case." And that was a salutary lesson.

When I absorbed that lesson, everything went grey and I found the Ancient Grandfather, high up a mountain side, crossing a dangerously unstable scree slope. I took a couple of steps; there was no doubt that disturbing the rocks could cause an avalanche and we would fall. The Grandfather guided me, and we cautiously made our way to the ridge above the scree, then on up the precipitous mountain.

When we reached the top, we came into the presence of a looming dark Eagle Spirit which made a move towards me; an action that was very awe-inspiring and scary. I considered fleeing to the arms of the Grandfather, but I realized that he had brought me to this place, that he was there behind me, and so I had nothing to fear. If there was danger, he would step in and save me, so I determined, not just to stand my ground, but to step forwards. I did step forward.

The Eagle Spirit overwhelmed me. Pitch black with what seemed to be holes in its body and carrying, in its talons, perhaps, bunches of lightning flashes. The lightning flashes looked something like the branches of a burnt-out tree, charred and black; if they were not lighting flashes, I couldn't imagine what they were. They distributed themselves all over my body so that I was all broken in pieces and no longer one homogeneous whole.

Behind the Eagle Spirit, I felt the presence of the Great Spirit and I called out to that Being. I felt the Great Hand touch me, felt the pressure on my body, and the feeling flowed into my navel centre, travelled up through my energy centres and out via my head centre. The Eagle Spirit stayed still. The Eagle Spirit is not the Great Spirit; it stands before the Great Hand that makes everything. I lost my fear of the Eagle and became very calm. I worried for a moment about the passing of time and the Eagle said: "There is no Time." I knew that this was true.

I understood that in the spirit world there is no Time and that is why the Love which comes from there is constant, does not judge, and is available whenever I can reach out to find it. This gave me great confidence and a strong feeling of connection to something outside of Time. I stayed with that feeling while it changed my body. Places of awareness popped into existence which had been closed to me before.

I began to be aware of noise in my body; a noise I recognised as spirits coming into my awareness, and, having thought about it for a bit, I decided to give them permission to be there. Although I must have already given permission in some realm of my Being, I have not articulated it before, so today I did invite them in but I asked them not to be so noisy and to be patient with me so that I can learn to understand them. I felt that everything would be alright and that I could take the Overwhelming.

In the dark intensity of the Eagle Spirit, I prayed for purity, for purity of my intentions so that nothing in my psyche would damage the work. In my navel centre I saw the pure silver circle of the Moon; this is the place where purity could be found.

Becoming the Power

Last night we watched a programme on Bears that have become dependent on human rubbish. They eat and eat and put on fat. Unlike humans, they can put on fat without damaging their metabolism and can become very, very heavy. Because of the continuous supply of food in the rubbish, they do not hibernate properly (I was going to say 'meditate'!). By adopting this easy lifestyle, they end up getting shot because they become an urban nuisance. All this happens because of human encroachment and that finishes them off.

I didn't feel very happy when I woke up. I came to meditate, and the spirits gripped me hard, not usually unbearable, but I was hurting. I tried to search for a meaningful connection. I went through many things, all of them powerful, all of them interesting, but none of them would move. For example, I arrived in yellow light; it was stunning and strong, but I found no .... what shall I say? No journeying there.

The image of a stone cube came very strongly, and it reminded me of geometry. I decided: "I'll just think about the shape." But this was, ... I was going to say sterile and academic, but I will say instead that I didn't want to use my mind in that way, and I tried to switch off.

Suddenly, I saw the traffic symbol for a roundabout, a triangular-shaped sign containing the graphic of a circle, a circle with gaps indicating exit roads. I arrived at the roundabout and went around it several times trying to decide which exit to take. I couldn't decide whether to go straight on, or to turn left, so I circled the roundabout getting more and more into pain in my lower centres.

A young Black Bear arrived. The roundabout was at the centre of his belly. The Bear said: "Why not go to the centre?" So that is the direction I headed in. Still I was lost for a long time as the conflicting image of the lazy urban Bear collided with the nurturing cosmic Mother Bear that I had met once before.

After a very long while, a sensation of my partner came. I felt there was something that had to be done in our relationship; there was something to release which was causing me to be stuck. At first, I blamed him, but then I saw his heart centre and I got the impression that I had to travel there. I fought hard against the idea; I was afraid it would take me back to where I had been for so many years. But then I realized there was no option, and I travelled forward. To my surprise, it was very pleasant to travel through his heart. I experienced his good side, and the love that he could express was visible to me there.

I came out the other side, finding myself still to be within the young Bear and noticing a great hole in my own body in the area of my lower centres. The Bear said to me, bluntly: "You are lost." I agreed: "I am lost." ..... After thinking about it for a minute, I continued: "But, Bear, is it such a bad thing if I am lost?"

There was a dramatic shift. The Bear and I were standing on the ridge of the dangerous scree, the ridge which leads up the steep mountain. The Bear indicated to me that I was right, it was not such a bad thing to have lost my I, and we made our way up to the top of the mountain.

The Bear said: "Look at the Thunder Being." The Eagle's body was dark, dark black. It bent its head, a head so big that the yellow beak covered me from my eye centre to my solar plexus and my body became a yellow bar like an ingot of gold. The energy centres on the wings of this Being became the ball joints of my shoulders, the right one was green and the left one was blue, and my shoulder joints were spirals. Below, in my navel centre the colour of the red was pure, and, because it was fluid, it was without geometry. I stayed with the Thunder Eagle for as long as I could, feeling totally released from my turmoil and my anxiety. I was waiting. I heard the word: 'Wait'. And I would wait.

I had such a wonderful day yesterday walking on the Fell that I am surprised I am so lost. I am not lost when I am talking directly to the spirits, but I am, kind of, lost in my life, lost to my life.

Grandfather, Ancient Grandfather, please help me to recall and record the details of this journey. When I woke this morning, I knew that the spirits were here and that an important journey would happen, at last. After three or four days of waiting, of my psyche not being ready, now it was. As soon as I began to meditate, I saw the alert, piercing and penetrating eye of the bird that is the most magnificent of all birds; I saw the eye of the Eagle. It is the most magnificent of birds because it comes and takes me directly into the presence of Great Spirit.

The Eagle took flight and I discovered that I myself had wings. I thought: "I had better follow." I flew after the Eagle and eventually it brought me to one particular place on the Sun Moon Dance field in England from which a very amazing view of a field of Maize had been visible. I was so surprised and so attracted by this field of green Maize, which is rarely grown in England, that, before the dance started, I went and lay there among the tall stalks of corn. The Eagle brought me to this green spot again and then it began a spiral ascent. In its talons it held an ear of ripe Maize and the individual seeds were falling off the cob, falling through the air in a yellow-gold cascade, falling towards me. My solar plexus centre was open; I caught them in my solar plexus, and I made sure that I collected them all. In among the falling seeds I saw a small smooth yellow Snake, like them it fell into my solar plexus. I knew there must be a black Snake similar. There was, and it fell in too.

These two caught Snakes entwined themselves around each other. In the circles formed between the spirals of their bodies I saw colours: the colour Green in the upper circle, in the circle below it the colour Blue. In the next circle there was a gap. In the circle below the gap I saw the colour Red, and in the final circle, Orange. I said the colours to myself so that I would have the order exact: Green, Blue, a gap, Red, Orange.

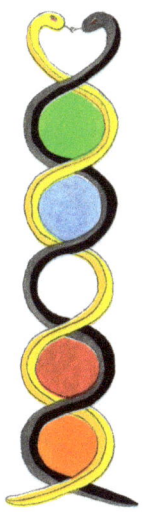

entwined snakes

I looked. I waited. I did not move with my own mind. I waited until the spirits moved me, and slowly, slowly I entered these colours.

I travelled into the Green, into my centre of seeing. The Green was the ability to see the great Grass Plains. I saw the plains with Buffalo scattered there, grazing.

From the Green, I was moved into the Blue: "Is this the Sky?" In reply, I heard: "Do not let the thoughts of your mind interrupt the teaching." And so, I just looked at the Blue. I saw the V-shaped tail of a marine creature. A Dolphin was idling, nose down, in the water so that all I could see was the tail waving. This was enough to tell me that the blue was the Ocean.

I noticed that the Blue was located in my throat centre and below it, in the heart centre, there was a gap, nothing wrong with this. It was not a place of travelling. It was a place of non-separation, non-being, non-seeing; it was empty of everything and without colour.

The Red was below that gap, and I really expected to travel into the Red. But no, the colour Orange came. I accepted this because it came so strongly and I knew that at other times when I have journeyed in the energy centres the connections between them are not only in a vertical line, but they connect in many ways which are neither vertical nor horizontal. I can travel from one to the other without any problem because of these incomprehensible connections.

I travelled into the Orange. I was nailing a piece of driftwood to a wall. It had that smoothed appearance and those special colours, of rusty black and beige, which come from being a long time in the Ocean. In the colour Orange, I heard myself say: "This is the place where I really exist." The Orange was the navel centre.

Now the journey becomes difficult to follow, but, somehow, I must have entered the Red. And now, this is where I am confused, because I see the Sun Moon Dance arbour in England, and I see a red ribbon. I see myself standing in my place asking: "What is this ribbon?" I see myself looking to the Tree, trying to see the ribbon of red running down the Tree and towards me along the track I made, like a red tongue uncurling. But this image did not have power.

So, I ran the colour Red the other way, from my own body towards the Tree, and the power of the dreaming focused. The colour Red was my solar plexus. I was on my belly dragging myself towards the Sun Moon Dance Tree, leaving a trail of the colour Red where my solar plexus was in touch with the earth; making that trail with blood because the rough ground was tearing the flesh, making it bleed.

The Grandfather of the Volcano appeared, and the dance arbour became composed of black and red spokes; red where the dancers gave of themselves in the dance and jet black between. The ground around the Dance Tree rose, carrying the Tree with it, and this created the image of a volcanic cone. From the centre, a great column of molten lava, rushing from below and rising upwards, fired out of the Volcano in a continuous stream. Now I visualize that when the molten column falls onto the earth, it turns black, stops moving, and makes the landscape. The colour Red is making the place where we walk; the place where we experience.

This is the last day of my brief visit here at the bungalow, Fair View. Do I really have to leave this beautiful peaceful space and go back to my other life? How will that work out? Will I ever come back here? I woke up in the middle of the night and the Moon was shining upon me. Although tipped on its side, it seemed to be fairly divided in half and looked like a slanted heart centre. I felt waves of silver light coming from the Moon to touch me and, in myself, I felt intense love and gratitude.

I came to meditate this morning and I felt the spirits were close. I waited. After a while I saw a horizontal line with a circle resting above it in the centre. It appeared to me that this was a symbol of the Eagle soaring on outstretched wings. The Eagle Spirit began to teach me about the Power. It was a very complicated meditation, which I couldn't hold together logically, but I knew that it was coming from spirit power and I remembered Joseph's teaching: "Become the Power." I realized, with relief, that I had no desire to use or abuse the Power. I just didn't have that need. In fact, the only thing I knew how to do was to become the Power, and that was a finished subject, never again would I need to worry about my attitude to the Power.

I opened up to the Power and the Power came in to dream within me in modern metaphors. I didn't hold, as I don't seem to be able to hold, the memory of these metaphors but there were cookers and crumbs in the bottom of cookers, and cooking pans, and fast roads and many other modern images. It seems to me now that the Power wants me to dream in modern imagery. I innately understand the ancient images of the Power because I lived them already, but the modern life has never been lived before and it is a very different life to follow. Maybe that is why I can't appreciate the metaphors, because this life is so confusing, and, really, maybe only the spirits understand it. So, I just let the spirits formulate the Power within me while I, I suppose I enjoyed it.

I have been often upset and confused since I came back from Scotland, but today I felt the close presence of spiritual power, so when I began to meditate, I clung to that and I asked the Ancient

Grandfather to send me an image. Immediately, a small square silver box came and, yes, the impulse was in my mind to reject it and look for another image, but luckily, I overcame that urge which seems to be the moment when the imagination will supersede the spiritual input. The personal self will seek for another image. Why? Because it is dissatisfied with the look of a very simple square box.

So, I grabbed that box firmly with my attention. I put it in the centre of my awareness, low down in my navel centre, and I looked intently at it. That is all that is required. It is very simple really, too simple for my modern mind which wishes to chase off and begin to make things up. But I know now, very well, the difference between the made-up thing and the Power-generated experience and so I was content to look at the silver box. Once I placed it in my navel, and once I laid my attention upon it, the problems of dissatisfaction went away. The box opened and inside was an eye. In my navel centre this eye was blue, then it moved to my solar plexus and the eye colour was brown. Many changes happened and everything began to go black.

I know that what I am going to say now is not exactly a faithful representation of the experience, but it is as near and as honest and as comprehensible as I can make it. I felt the Spirit of the Volcano come, black as pitch; this is the mysterious Father and Grandfather who is both he and she, and I pushed myself forwards into the blackness. Suddenly there was a radical alteration of place and I flew through the blackness of space towards a single silver Star and, as I travelled, I noticed that when the silver starlight twinkles red, the Red is something feminine, and when the starlight twinkles blue, the Blue is something masculine.

When the Red and the Blue collide, the result is an explosion of volcanic proportions. Up there in the Stars there are many massive explosions going on. I saw how the Blue-Red Spirit is indeed the Spirit of Explosions. Yes, this mysterious and daunting Spirit took me through the deep blackness of the night sky to a silver Star. Now once I had myself been to a Star, not quite like this today. Today it was about the power of, I would say: "Big bangs in the Universe."

I must have become restless, because I heard: "Being and doing are forbidden here." I had to simply observe and, of course, being an observer and not a participator is why I can hardly remember anything; I was neither doing nor being, so my memory was not active. I was surprised, then, to become aware in my heart centre which was filling with the most glorious warm yellow light, and here again was a place of neither doing nor being. The right wing of the Thunder Eagle came into my vision. The wing was lying unfurled near shallow water and the vortex on the wing was clearly visible. The three feathers at the end of the wing were very long and the tips were touching the water, so that, when this Being took flight, drops of water would shower down from them.

I wanted to pause during this journey and do the usual fixing process to bring more of it back, but the opportunity for this was not given me. I think it was a test of my willingness to surrender, and I passed that test because I willingly followed the Spirit of the Volcano and tried to learn those ways which are very different to ways that I am familiar with.

I feel totally inept and I expect the spirits are laughing, but I did see a vision. I saw the thinnest, thinnest green line lying on and bending with the curve of the horizon of the Earth. Below was black and Above was black, black earth and black sky, and, between them was the thinnest, thinnest line of luminescent green. A Silver Being came from space and changed something.

When I came to meditate again, I knew that all the conditions were right, and it was down to me to overcome the parts of myself which work against connection. When I had played the drum the night before I knew, as I often know, that I am the weak link here in this modern world. The spirits are constant, benevolent, outside of Time, always sending the healing power in a constant stream, but I am confused in the dynamic of daily life, often confused.

The Power began to enter my awareness in a physical way, to actually enter my body, and I understood that what I needed to do today was to allow the Power to move through my great body into every cell of my Being. I cannot speak in words, or understand in words, or know in words what the Power is and how it works, but, if I allow it to enter every cell of my body, my body will remember and the Power will be stored there, and so I did this.

It began in my navel centre and, radiating outwards from there, it moved up my body. When it came to my heart, I felt tickling in my throat and I knew the barrier at the throat was still in place, perhaps not as completely dammed up as it used to be, but certainly still a blockage that has to be released. I determined that, before the Power got there, I would relax my throat centre and I tried to do this. However, the Power passed from my heart to my head and into my centre of seeing, bypassing the throat.

In the eye centre, I became aware of the great White Eagle; the Eagle which stands alone and is complete in its self; the Eagle whose feathers are strangely soft, shaped like crescent moons and slippery, close to fluid; very different to an Eagle in this world. I surrendered completely to the presence of the White Eagle until it filled my awareness. This took some time and when it was finished the blackness of the Eagle wings from Uluru came. The White

Eagle, pure spirit, I had not encountered in this world; it had not come to me in a physical body, but the Wedge-tailed Eagles had come to me in Australia.

As I left the White Eagle, the barrier in my throat centre was swept away and my throat opened wide; the blockage had gone, and I breathed the air of spirit into my body. The air expanded my body and also made sound through my throat and mouth to facilitate correct speaking because that is what needs to be achieved. In this way I travelled into the black Eagle-ness to the Spirit of the Volcano, who I had once heard called, 'Black Eagle' and, at that time, had tried to avoid. Now I was absolutely certain that this Spirit is a most important guiding spirit for me, and this Spirit became so huge in my awareness, leaving only a small space at the right-hand side, that nothing could have been more convincing.

Suddenly a group of us, human beings, were breaking up the cage that used to be the safe house for my little rabbit on the lawn. We pulled off all the wire netting and then we broke up the wooden frame. I heard this: "Now we will take responsibility." I opened my eyes. I looked at the round lampshade on the ceiling light, a painted paper world, blue sky with clouds and a rainbow, and I knew that the responsibility which had been taken was for the health of the planet.

Now, in my mind which struggles in the everyday, I would say how ridiculous this idea is, but at that moment it was utterly correct. There was a way that in my Being I was capable of caring for the planet and I presume that is what the great physical awareness of the Power today was about; certainly I felt it in so many parts of my Being and was aware of it entering my cells and knew that it would be held in the memory of the individual cells of my body. I won't bore myself with saying again how far this description is from the experience, but I hope when I recall it that it will inspire me to go further: that is the point of all of this.

The spirit voices said: "Welcome to the metaphors of the modern world" and I was a pie in a glass dish with pastry below but no pastry on top. The centre of this pie contained stewed apples with a little bit of icing sugar spread over them. Apples are the seasonal fruit at the moment, and, maybe, that is why apples were used, or maybe apples were used because they make a fairly colourless puree.

This pie was being carried towards a table by invisible hands, carried towards a great feast. I was changing radically, and I felt fear; would my concentration be sufficient, or would I fall from that place of consciousness? The voices said to me: "This pastry cannot fall." I saw the image of the hands carrying the dish and I knew what they said was true. I allowed myself to enter the very radically altered state.

I have just forgotten where I was, but the pie, I think, was being carried to the feast, and I was allowing my mind to enter into the extremely altered state which becoming a pie takes you to, when I saw the barrier. The barrier was horizontal and the entrance to the other place was through a crack so minute I didn't think I could get through it. I called out for help; a small Flatworm came, one of those jet-black Flatworms you see in the bottom of ponds. Travelling in the body of this creature, the journey through the horizontal crack was easy and I came into another world.

As I entered this world I exclaimed with shock: "This is a no-place!" I wondered how I knew, but indeed, as I regained my shape and looked around, it was the case. And then I saw the beak of the

Thunder Being. Next moment I was torn in half. Out of the central tear something fell. It was me and I fell away into nothing. In the no-place there was no thing and there was no me. But .....

I saw balls of colour dropping through a great universal space. At the bottom of their fall they were caught in a net which was my awareness. The net stretched and then bounced back, and the balls flew back up through space again, Blue and Red and Yellow. That was a very amazing image. If my net had not been there would they just have passed through this space and travelled on forever? And, what was the point of the net which caught the coloured balls of light and bounced them back again? I don't know, but it had something to do with being within the energy field of the Thunder Being.

Within the Thunder Being, the state of awareness was very different, and I could feel my spirit body quite acutely. Blue Light had replaced my me-ness and I prayed to maintain the Blue Light and to be stable in the Blue Light. Then, as I came out of that state, my spirit awareness was dizzy and falling. As I fell, I came back into my physical awareness and Green Light replaced the Blue. I can't say any more now, except: "Thank you, spirits, and help me to pursue the right course." And, because it makes me happy to do this, not to think that I have no right to be happy and therefore destroy the work, which seems to be, bringing joy into the world.

When I played my wooden flute last night, I got such pain in my navel centre and solar plexus that in the end I lay face down on the floor and connected in to the earth; I was understanding some things about being open to receiving the deep earth energy in a healing capacity.

I woke in the night to the presence of Love. The Spirit of Love was here, touching me, and it was beautiful. I woke this morning and came to meditate, and that Spirit returned. The yellow light of the sunrise was filling the sky as I came to meditate, and it was beautiful. I travelled with Love and I was reminded of what I have learnt about why human beings, myself included, are so attracted to negative thinking. It is because the acute sensitivity of feeling that comes with love brings with it all the suffering in the world and it is not possible to be immune to those sufferings. I understand this now.

I kept asking questions and at this stage of a meditation a question destroys utterly, utterly destroys, the connection to the incoming Spirit. I managed to move away from the questions and be carried by Love into some very altered states. At one point the power of Love slowly rose up my body, coming to rest in my meditative eye, and I felt my face disappearing. I understood the metaphor of the Face, which is a barrier between one thing and another, and my face disappeared. I entered into the Spirit that was around me and I travelled.

I saw the Thunder Eagle as one great golden-yellow sphere, and, as I travelled towards it, I knew there are five spheres emanating from that Being and that they are the vibrations which make the created world. All the five spheres of light were yellow-gold from a distance, but as I approached them they took up their individual colour vibrations. I found myself travelling towards the sphere of the right shoulder of the Great Bird and I entered the Green. The Bird folded its wings around all the emanations which condensed into the centre of its Being into one great ball of vibrating Purple Light and in that light, Joseph was carried.

The Heart of the Father

The week after I closed my business I rewarded myself for twenty-five years of hard work with a course at the local Falconry Centre, although it was only the end of October snow fell, and consequently I spent a wonderful time on my own with the teacher of the course because nobody else who had booked came. Oh, it was cold, and the weather was appalling, but I enjoyed every minute and I came home with my eyes full of beautiful birds. I had a lot of pain sitting in front of the fire that night and felt quite worried about my state of health, yet I did not feel downhearted, I felt inspired to do what I could to seek out if I had any healing gifts to help others.

The next morning, I came to meditate. The black Eagle Spirit was standing to my right. I thought of all the living Eagles I met yesterday; although they all had Eagle spirits and this too was an Eagle Spirit, this Spirit was like none of them. I recalled some meditations where this Eagle Spirit had been very looming, very overwhelming, and very present, meditations where I felt some fear of this Spirit and wondered what it was, and meditations where I travelled within it and was changed in there. I remembered that I had decided not to fear the Eagle in this form, to make the effort to willingly know it, join with it, become in it, and bring the knowledge of it back here. I prayed for help. I prayed for my house here in England to sell so that I can go to Scotland and do this work. I saw clearly my bedroom at Fair View and the Power came in extraordinary quantities in that place and my whole body here became hotter and hotter and broke out into a sweat.

Suddenly there was a great change and my voice, strong, calm and knowing completely what it wanted and what was required, spoke. My voice said: "I want to travel to the heart of the Father." We travelled and I saw a particular shape; a black circle, and, below it, two lines descending at an angle to each other, the gap between them widening as they went. The third line was more horizontal and bent downwards in the middle; this bent line crossed the descending lines. The shape made in the centre of these three lines was a diamond whose top was more pointed than the bottom. Outside the centre, between the extending bent line and the continuing descending lines, two angles were formed that held small black diamond-shapes, one on either side. The diamond centre of this geometric figure was blue. This was the entrance to the heart of the Father, and we went through.

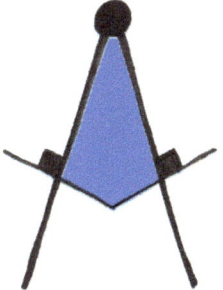

the heart of the father

Within the heart of the Father were four more shapes, one below the other, forming a column. They were similar to the initial shape but not the same; the circle at the top had gone and upward extending crossed lines were there instead, so that these shapes looked like structures whose energy lines penetrated the earth and reached towards the sky, connecting below and above. The uppermost one of these structures had a blue interior. The next one, which was connected to the heart of my self, was red. The next one was green, and the bottom one was again blue.

The spirits sent me to the green shelter, and this was the place of healing for the physical body. There are a lot of things to know about these four shelters and maybe I will learn more. Today I knew that the Green healed the physical body and I was there. I think the Red heals the spiritual body, and I think the Blue above and the Blue below are the Sky and the Sea which are the expressions of the Blue Spirit of healing in the World. So, these colours, Blue, Red, Green, Blue, are at the heart of the Father.

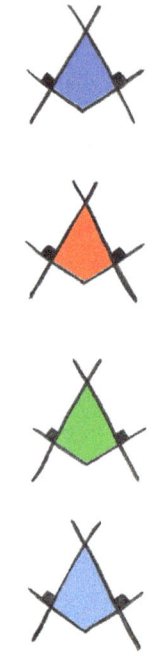

4 shelters

Then I heard: "Something will come into the world through you to help." It was about to happen at that moment, and it did happen. I felt myself to be the outer edge of an energy circle and something was coming through, but I felt it wasn't my business to know what the help was, and I did not attempt to discover anything about it. On the way back, the spirits helped me to remember some of the details so that I could record them here. And, as they brought me back into this place, they said: "Be as you are."

Be As You Are

Last night I really enjoyed playing the wooden flute, it has a lovely warm and breathy tone. As I played, I became aware of a bright yellow light high in the right side of my vision. The light was so intense that I wondered what it was. Could it be a reflection of the candle flame cast on the wall, but how could that be so bright? I quickly determined not to look in that direction. Searching for a proof that it was spirit light or desiring to prove that it only existed in the physical world, either action would take me far from making music, so I shut my eyes and continued to play. Later I took up the drum and sang a song to the spirits asking them to help me to be better than I think I am.

I came to meditate this morning aware that a Spirit was already with me; the Spirit of the Ancient Grandfather had come to me and given me the energy to get out of bed in this cold house and get myself organised. When I began to meditate, I travelled through red and blue noticing that, whatever pattern these colours appeared in today, red always came first. Then I realized that I was travelling fast into my left-hand awareness. Far to the left, a black horizon was visible on the Great Plains and above it there was an immense cloud of blackness, a great Thundercloud in the sky, and this was the daunting and impressive body of the black Eagle Spirit occupying the West.

Suddenly with a kind of bang, or a pop, I saw a black figure standing closer to me. It was an aspect of Joseph, not the fun loving, caring, selfless Joseph who teaches us on Earth, but a quiet and calm black Joseph that, huh-huh, resides in the Thundercloud. I can't think how to describe it better than that without making it sound as if he is created by the Thundercloud. It is just that, that aspect of him is visible within the sphere of influence of the Thunder Being. Some Purple Light began to play, and I understood how the Purple Light belongs to the storm clouds.

Oh, think how Joseph did it! .... Being with this Spirit of Joseph, my awareness became more central and I became aware in my solar plexus at the centre of my body. Strange, things are jumbled up now, because I saw this solar plexus hole and wind, straight from the Void, was blowing out of it. Black and yellow fringes attached to the edge of the hole, were blown like long hair in my direction, so that I saw them, like streamers waving in the breeze, stretching towards me. Then I saw something very strange in that space which was like a little upturned funnel. We used to have something like it in the workroom for putting oil into the machines. I looked at this upside-down funnel sitting there, not really having a clue what it was about.

I think the funnel was just a diversion, because suddenly invisible spirits carried a sacred bundle into my space. This bundle was all wrapped up in muslin, an insubstantial white cloth which billowed in the wind. They unwrapped this object to reveal the trunk of a tree. I bent forward to touch it and the tree became the australian Sun Moon Dance Tree planted in the arbour in the State of Victoria. I, as a dancer, was the lower half of the Tree, the part that had been stripped bare. It was up to me to hold the Tree in the ground and I put my arms around it. This image produces the vision of White below and Blue above; myself as the White dancing and stamping on the ground to keep the Tree firm and to enliven the Earth, and the Chief bringing the Power down from the Blue sky.

I needed to go further, and I felt very ill, but I was encouraged to pass through the barrier, which was caused by my reluctance to admit something: 'admit' in the sense of 'to let something in'. With that encouragement, I passed through the barrier and it became clearer to me what was entailed in the Sun Moon Dance process. I stored that knowledge.

They brought me to the shores of a lake; the surface of this lake was like a silver mirror. They said to me: "You are the surface of this lake." The silver mirror intensified the colour of the blue sky and this was the perfection of what was required to be done by the people, and I did this.

Then I said: "Where is my reward?" It was a deep shock to hear myself make this demand, but I realized that I was honestly expressing something: "Where is my reward? I don't think I can do this work without a reward." I felt that the effort of doing it was so great that when I came back, I would be reluctant to go again, and my physical self would put obstacles in the way of my being able to get there. It was my physical self that craved a reward.

I struggled with this for a while, then, of course, I got a guilty conscience about requesting a reward. Really, the point was that I had realized it would always be difficult to cross the barriers to do such work and that was a daunting challenge for me. I was analysing the situation and the spirits reminded me: "Don't let your observations disrupt the process." It was important that I observed what was going on and had some memory of it, but I had to be careful not to insert my ideas and, by doing that, change the course of the experience that was coming to me. That is the technique which I am trying to learn at the moment: to cross the pain barriers when they come without any reward, to observe without interpreting, to bring back the memory with as little interference as possible from myself, and put it on the tape in order to be inspired to travel further by listening to my experiences at a later date.

I thank Joseph and the Thunder Being for giving me such a task, and I understand much more clearly the relationship between the dancers and the Chief, especially as the dancer becomes more experienced. May the Blue and the Silver Lights work together for the benefit of all the people.

U-uu

carrying

Standing Together

After my third Sun Moon Dance I left the West and went to live in the North, in Scotland, but still my previous house had not sold and remnants of my connections in the West lingered on. One night, in my new home, I decided not to set my alarm and just sleep until I woke up. I woke about quarter to nine in the morning. I knew it was necessary for there to be a change in my meditation routine but it was a big battle, because I felt lazy on account of the fact that I didn't wake up to meditate at six, even though that was originally put in place because of my busy life style. So, trying not to panic, I came to meditate at about half past nine. I live completely alone now, so there was little chance of an interruption, still, I can't say I felt particularly connected to the spirit world, but I lay down.

Immediately my mental state changed, and I began to feel the incoming spiritual presences. I moved towards them and I began to see parts of the Thunder Eagle. This Being is so big that I cannot encompass it with my awareness all in one go. I would see the hooked beak; I would travel further, and I would see a part of a leg. Only after the feathers of the wings had pushed against my solar plexus and I had felt there the tough and sharp feathers of the Eagle, did I know that I was within the Great Bird, and that, by coming into me, I had been absorbed into it.

The space inside was very large. I looked around and seeing Joseph standing there in the emptiness, I approached him. I saw purple and I also saw, low down, the pale blue colour that he has been showing me recently. I looked down into the Blue, and far, far, far away and far, far, far, far down I saw a brilliant spot of silver light. Joseph communicated to me without words that I should travel to this silver light and I did so. It was way down, almost beyond the feet of the Thunder Eagle. As I approached, it shone like a diamond. Maybe it would be a multi-faceted diamond but, when I got very close, it was not: it was a flat object with concave sides. It was like a small cutting tool, like a double-ended chisel, but it was made of silver light.

As I looked at the silver light, something changed, the spirits announced: "The about-to-be-born" and they opened a door. Through the open door I saw the inside of a Church and a stone font brimming with water. Although I was born into a christian society, I had rejected the religion when I was fifteen. I spoke out: "I do not want to see this. I do not want to see christian power. Why has this been chosen?" In response, the power of the carved stone font and the power of the water came into me. Then the spirits showed me Jesus Christ. I was fighting this set of images. I was fighting when they showed me Jesus Christ, and then they said: "Jesus was Love and he failed."

While they were showing me this unwelcome vision, I had noticed the Ancient Grandfather, standing to the right, watching the scene. Well, when they had finished showing me, I had had enough of that extremely strong experience which I would in no way have sought for myself, and I ran to the Grandfather to hide behind him. He was wearing a long robe of Buffalo skin. I put my head against it, my eyes popped open and I was back.

What can I glean from the christian images and the statement the spirits made? The power of the stones and the power of the water were undeniable. The beauty of the message of unconditional love that Jesus taught is undeniable. Perhaps the point was, that Jesus failed because the conditions were such that he was bound to fail. Nothing was said about whether the Spirit of Pure Love would succeed the next time it entered our place.

I went to Australia a second time, to dance and to fulfil a task that Joseph had given me: to bring the White ribbon, one of the four colours which were tied round the Tree at the first dance, back to the second dance; in this way carrying the intention that the dance would continue in Australia.

Before the dance I travelled along the Great Ocean road, with a dear friend, discovering the mighty nature of the Southern Ocean. We found such a beautiful, peaceful place to stay that we stopped for two days and on the second morning, when I came to meditate, many images of the foaming breakers I watched the day before came back to me. We had visited a place where the Ocean cut under the land for many metres, a large sink hole had appeared where waves rushed and crashed into that deep dead end, an awe-inspiring and frightening sight. As I had done the day before, I came down the steps cut in the rock that led into the hole carved by the relentless motion of the sea. I knew this was dangerous, but it was also exciting. Now I went back to stand with the person who accompanied me in my meditation, my Teacher, and, while the waves ebbed and flowed, we listened to the roaring. I think he admired my courage in going forwards, but it was better for us to stand together.

His Eagle's wing came to me, with it came the memory of how he had handed it to me at the last seminar to hold while he prepared to give someone a healing. When he was ready, I handed it back to him and he said: "Good." This meant that I had held it right, thought the right thoughts, and brought some power in. Then I saw the black Eagle wings. The energy of those wings was very different. My Teacher's brown wing was full of love and healing. The black wings had a different feeling and the power in them was unknown to me. With my right hand I picked up and held the wing that would be most comfortable in that hand. The colour Red was with this wing and I saw red ribbons on the handle. I took up the other wing, the colour Blue was there, and that wing would be for the left hand. I had an impression that I knew what they would do. The Red wing would heal by bringing the feeling of the Power to the person who was being cleansed. The Blue wing, on the other hand, would cleanse their personality and enable them to be free of trauma, to be empty; it would be healing in that way. One would bring gifts and the other would take pains away.

I came to meditate this morning. Straight away I saw the Thunder Being. Straight away the energy centre that is its body attached to my body and I travelled towards the energy centre of its head. With surprise, I discovered that Being has only one eye. I travelled into the eye. Radical shifts in my body awareness were happening and it was up to me to be empty so that these things could happen. Not to cut off those feelings because of some unhappiness which had affected my life but to be free from the interpersonal clamps that hold consciousness in the daily world; be free of those and allow my body to become hollow and to feel the ripples of the Power dissolving away any blocks in consciousness which inhibit the flow. I was extraordinarily surprised at the great privilege which was being bestowed upon me while knowing that it came through the Sun Moon Dance.

Moving inside the Thunder Eagle I met a Red Squirrel. What was a creature which lives in dense woodland doing there? Next, I met a Silver Salmon, a creature which migrates up the streams to breed. I said to the Squirrel and the Salmon: "Surely the Eagle has torn you apart and eaten you?" And the Squirrel told me that was how they came to dwell within it. Those creatures were there to help me; they too had been consumed by the Eagle and lived within the great body in that space of awareness and freedom which exists within the Eagle's orb.

I asked myself: "What does the Squirrel do?" And I answered: "The Squirrel collects nuts and stores them for the winter." The Squirrel told me: "Yes, I am your memory within the Eagle otherwise you will become so enraptured by the Power that nothing will go back in your memory to the other place." "Thank you, Red Squirrel. You are so busy and so beautiful!" I looked at the Salmon, at the streamlined body covering the pink flesh that would be exposed when the Eagle's talons ripped its silver skin.

A strange scene was there of an ancient Oak tree whose branches hung over the banks of the stream. I heard that the Salmon and the Squirrel live on the Oak berries; that is what the acorns were called; they were not called acorns, they were called

Oak berries. The Squirrel collected them from the tree and the land, the ones that dropped into the stream were consumed by the Salmon. I was very surprised that the Salmon would eat acorns but nevertheless, I am left with the image of the Salmon eating the Oak berries and that is all I can say. That is how the Oak tree supports the Squirrel and the Salmon and they in turn support the Eagle. The Eagle swooped down, picked me up and flew into the sky.

As the Eagle climbed higher, lifted up by the power of its wings, the only creature in my travel today which could carry me upwards, I noticed that it had become a fishing Eagle with a white head and a black body. We flew up, up, up and, in the distance, I saw the cone-shaped black Mountain with the snow-covered crystal tip. The Eagle was taking me there, but the Eagle also was that Mountain: the metaphors came together. I looked again at this Mountain which I have visited before. The crystal tip was so tiny it could, perhaps, only be a few atoms. I recalled how I had travelled into it before. How could that have been when the crystal is so minute? But suddenly I must have been even smaller because the Crystal was right in front of me, big as a house. I walked in.

Once inside I began to pray. I began by apologising. I spoke to the Crystal Being and I said: "The first time I came here, I didn't want to know you and I turned away as you welcomed me. Now I long to be part of whatever you do, whatever you are doing, and I have come to be here and do the thing that is done by the Crystalline emanations."

I saw those Beings, tall, like waving fronds, almost C-shaped, by that I mean the letter 'c', and their heads, which they did not have because they were just like wisps or blades of grass, seemed to bend backwards and then they would bend forwards. They suggested that I kneel and put my head to the crystal floor and pray with them. They bent forwards and shouted out: "Hosanna!" I was quite surprised to hear that word. I said the word to myself very quietly: "H-oh" that syllable made sense to me; the sound of agreement and being prepared to be taught. "Z-ah n-ah" well, I don't know, but that is what those Crystalline Beings were calling out as they thanked the Creator, and I joined in with them in doing that.

Suddenly I could feel that my consciousness was in the Salmon. I was the Salmon swimming with my head pointing into the flow of the silver stream, feeling the clear crystal waters coursing over my scaly body, cleansing me and enabling me to breath. The Squirrel was there saying: "I will hold your memory, just BE in the flow." I put my head firmly into the flow of the cool clear purifying waters of the stream. I felt my lower body contract and I saw thousands of eggs exiting from my body in a great burst, and, as I gave everything in the production and release of those eggs, my consciousness travelled out in one of them. As they drifted and bounced in the current of the stream, the surface of those transparent eggs shimmered with the colours of the rainbow and, floating there in a great mass, they were beautiful. The flesh of the Salmon turned yellow, and, maybe, the Eagle pulled that weak Salmon out of the stream and ate her, or, maybe she made her way back to the Ocean to grow strong in order to return and perform this act of worship again.

I was in ecstasy in my journey there with the Crystal Beings calling to the Great Spirit: "Hosanna! Hosanna!" when the Eagle turned my head around and slowly steered me through the images of the journey back to this place, and on the way back I began to feel very ill. When the ill feeling got too much, which, I guess, was me hanging onto something that I could no longer have, I popped out of that place of consciousness. The last thing I saw was the Squirrel who had carried all the images back here for me.

Yesterday I finished writing my memories of the second Sun Moon Dance in the UK. Last night, late, I drew the picture for the front cover. Travelling in meditation this morning I saw those two Guardian Beings at the top of the Tree, staring steadfastly towards the East gate and protecting the arbour from intruders, behind them the Buffalo looking to the West.

Dance Tree

In the West, within the circle of the arbour, I noticed a square opening. I saw black and yellow, and I knew it was the entrance to the Thunder Being. When looking at that Being I find that I must not try to see a form, but I must try to observe the mystical, incomprehensible, formlessness of it which is distinguishable by the fact that it is the Black Light and the Yellow Light mixing and moving together.

I decided to walk through the square opening, but I did not want to go alone. I backed up towards the Tree, feeling the Tree strong against my spine, and, above me, the head of the Buffalo, hanging there, staring into the Void. I sent my attention up to the Buffalo skull. The love and the power of the skull poured down into my body. I felt that any moment I could rise and be taken away in the ecstasy of the Buffalo spirit. But I kept my feet upon the ground and did not allow my attention to wander from the swirling yellow and black vortex in the square hole.

I invited the Buffalo and the Sun Moon Dance Tree to enter the hole with me and the three of us went forward into the turbulence of the Yellow and Black Lights. The Buffalo skull assumed the form of the Black Buffalo and inside the vortex of the Thunder Being this previously inert Buffalo could move. He walked behind me and, when I was unable to move, pushed me forward gently, powerfully, inexorably.

I was carrying the Sun Moon Dance Tree on my back and I thought: "The Buffalo is helping me and knows what I need. What about the Tree?" I could make a crutch out of it, a stick which would help me propel myself along, or I could light it and use it as a torch so that I could see because the place we had entered was pitch dark. But I was content to be and to be moving in that place without light, and I did not want to use the Sun Moon Dance Tree as a crutch as if it was something which was merely there to support me.

I stopped thinking about what I might do and, returning my attention to the present moment, I found that the Tree and I were leaning at an angle of about forty-five degrees to the horizontal. We were halfway between lying down and standing up and we were becoming one. I raised my arms up so that they mirrored the Y-shape of the Tree; my head dropped forward and became the

Buffalo skull. The Black Buffalo, now only a skin, lay over us and formed a third layer of this sacrifice; myself below, the Tree in the centre, and the Buffalo surrounding us, but all of us One: my arms, the arms of the fork of the Tree; my head, the head of the Buffalo; my spine, the trunk of the Tree; my skin, the skin of the Buffalo.

In this way we travelled on, looking at the two lights and hearing that the Black Light of the Thunder Eagle is the creator of the Yellow Light. It is the great magical secret power and mystery of the Thunder Being that out of the Darkness came Light. I don't think anybody could understand or control this mystery and that is the greatness of the Being of Thunder.

I knew that the vision was over, but I was going to stay there in the delight of the deep mystery. Descending from above came red and blue lines of light, red to the left and blue to the right. I called out: "Father" because I knew the Spirit of the Volcano was coming in those lights and then I saw the cone of the black Mountain. The Volcano was erupting and the Blue and the Red Lights were shooting up the chimney of the volcanic cone and flying out into the atmosphere of the world. With those lights I came, and I came back to this place, in my roots still connected to the vision, which was given to me there, and wanting to be aware in that place of consciousness consciously, always.

The Rainbow

I felt overwhelmed by the Power. I lay down and entered a journey where I saw the hoof print of a horse in soft ground. I went to the grey mare, her ears twitched as I whispered: "I do love you; you know." Putting my arm across her shoulders I looked again at the hoof print and felt the power. I began to chant the word

'Joseph', not only chanting the vowels but chanting the consonants as well. The letters formed an arch, in the centre there was a circular hole filled with the colour Green, but it was not formed from the 'O' of 'Joseph': from the left 'J', 'O', and 'S' were placed in order up to the hole with 'E', 'P' and 'H' down the other side. After chanting and seeing the six letters of the name forming an arch, it was clear to me that I was looking at an image of a rainbow. I was trying to discover the insights in this picture when I recognised the shape of the horse's hoof in the bow of the rainbow, and a connection was made there between the power of the horse and the arc of the rainbow.

Joseph in the rainbow

As I chanted, leaving the spelling of the word and moving towards the sounds, the letters of Joseph's name slowly transformed to 'J-O-Z-E-F'. The meaning of the sounds came to me: 'seeing with eyes of innocence the connections between above and below creates the place of faith'. That is a beautiful name.

I don't remember the steps by which I came next to the place where I said: "I have no wants. I have no desires." But immediately I said that I felt the presence of the Eagle and I knew that I could only ever meet the Eagle in the place where I have no desires. I moved radically to the left into the experience on the road to Uluru when we stopped among the bodies of the dead Eagles.

I particularly went into the experience of picking up the body of the first Eagle we came across. I had held it up by the wing joints, pulling the body up in front of me; it had covered my whole torso and still its feet touched the ground. I had called to my Teacher: "Look at this Eagle!"

What happened in my meditation was that I became dressed in that Eagle as if it was garment which I had put on. As I stood there, the tattered and crushed body of the Eagle clothing me, I felt the Eagle Spirit come in behind me. I realized: "Something I left behind is entering into my experience now."

I moved, and I was walking into my empty heart centre. It seemed to me so right that the heart centre was full of emptiness. I know that people may feel unhappy about having an empty heart, but on the level of the energy centres in the meditative world the heart is empty because it is connected to the One. A spirit said to me, hum, what were the exact words? Not these, but this was the meaning: don't be afraid to be joined to people in the heart centre. I understood a new way of being in the empty heart where a loving connection is able to be still, not subject to change, trauma, or disturbing emotions.

I came to meditate this morning. Very soon the feeling of the young Black Bear was with me. The Bear was walking away from me, and I ran after him. Travelling with the Bear, there was a cloud of Purple Light, and when I looked into that Bear there was Joseph. The Bear was walking with a stick and he handed it to me. The stick was very long, thin and black, more like a piece of plastic rod than a stick made of wood, and just a few inches taller than me. At the top was a little horizontal bar about four inches wide which was yellow.

the stick

When the Bear gave his stick to me, I put the horizontal bar to my centre of seeing; the stick entered my body through my eye centre and began to travel down. I felt like a sword swallower. I watched its progress and I noticed that it would soon come to the point where my legs split my body in half. I thought: "Hum? What's it going to do when it gets there? Is it going to stop dead at that point?" But it did not. When it reached that point, it split, and the two lines of the split stick went down to the ground. And so it was that the yellow horizontal line came to be two feet, and the split section of the black vertical line became my legs.

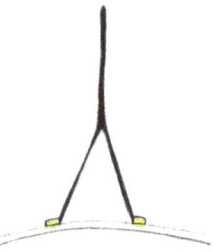

legs and feet

The straight black legs began to bow outwards and between them they formed an arch. Where the legs joined, there was a

central hole,

the hole in the centre

and here was a most strange image of the rainbow; with the centre hole as the base, the remaining seven circles of the energy centres were piled in a vertical column, and I dreamed into them the colours of the rainbow.

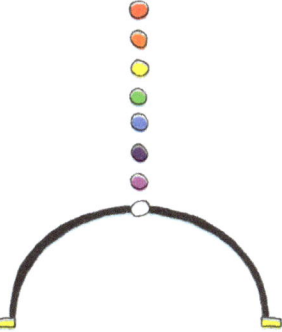

piled rainbow

I looked at the energy centres coloured in this way and slowly things changed. The rainbow of Joseph, the beautiful painted arrow, seemed to me to emanate from the green centre of the seven-coloured bow created by raindrops and sunlight. I looked again at the clear circle at the base of the column of the piled rainbow; an opening into which I seem to be able to look with clarity but there was no travelling there today. The rainbow enfolded that circle and the colours formed concentric rings around the openness of the centre. I felt that it was by means of the colours of the rainbow that anything at all was able to be experienced in the emptiness and that once the rainbow colours encircled the hole then the world of experience was made. That was the impression I got from the images that I was seeing.

emanations from the centre

I am seeing again the concentric lights of the rainbow encircling the world. This rainbow is created by the Thunder Eagle. The stick is a representation of the lightning energy that runs down through my body in a flash, grounding me to the earth with legs and feet and bringing the rainbow teachings to seed experience in the essential emptiness of the, now green, field of Below.

Time Steps

Yesterday was the day of the Fire Ceremony, held on the seventh of each month, to honour the Oceans. In the building, the lighting, and the watching of the fire there is cleansing and purification for the waters and the people.

I came to meditate this morning. I was gripped and very soon I saw the Eastern gate of the medicine wheel and a yellow Eagle entering through that gate. As the Eagle became more and more present, I heard a voice say: "Transcend the barriers of Time." I thought to myself: "Well, this must be what the Eagle is all about."

I was thrown into the dark and yet the yellow Eagle was still clearly visible. I became more and more aware of the body of the Eagle. My personal consciousness was resting somewhere in the chest area, and my perception was emanating from there into the Eagle's head as it gradually entered and energised my upper centres.

The spirits had said: "Transcend the barriers of Time" but I was very intent upon becoming the Eagle and I decided that I would continue with this for a while. When I say 'a while' I mean as many meditations as it takes, or are sent to me, until somehow, with the help of the Eagle, I will go through a barrier out of Time and into the Timeless. From that moment on it will be the case that my daily life will not be disconnected from the place where Time does not exist.

So, I settled within the awareness of the Eagle watching the unfolding of the becoming. In this process the Eagle turned from yellow to brown and a square opening to an underground room became visible. I recalled the meeting with the brown Eagle fixed to the T-shaped stand. I remembered that I had interpreted this experience as an initiation taking place in the spirit world; this gave me more confidence to continue what I was doing today.

The brown Totem Eagle, now free to move, began to descend in steps that were shaped like T-s, not the easiest thing for a grounded Eagle to accomplish. I watched these steps descend; as they appeared, they looked, to me, something like the individual frames of a projected motion picture.

The T-shape is the stand of the Eagle and the T-shape is a symbol of Time. Steps of Time descending: that is what I saw.

Time steps

If Time comes in descending steps, then I need to climb upwards to reach the Ancestors.

Yes, I will surrender myself and step into the Eagle and, in this way, be one day free of Time, or perhaps, none day free of Time. So difficult to describe, but the Eagle has been waiting for a long time. When I came back to this world of every day, I burned up with the most fearsome heat. I was advised to drop my concentration on my physical discomfort and float through into the nothingness. This is what I did, and then, in a few moments, I was back here quite ok if, perhaps, a little spaced out.

Some days later I lay down to meditate for a while. The black wings came to me and I felt it was time to take them off the top of the wardrobe and begin to work with them, time to bring them out into the open. Then suddenly, as it seemed to me, the Thunder Eagle placed a word in front of my eyes. This word was 'Hello'.

I suppose I had been thinking about my time with Joseph, remembering that part of the work, we are called to do, is to enliven the metaphors of our modern languages; to explore the levels of meaning in the language we use, in the way that he has shown us exists in the language of his Ancestors, and here, now, was the word 'Hello'.

As if to encourage me, the echoing of voice of the Eagle thundered in my mind, helping me to resonate with the word 'Hello', and I found that the greeting 'Hello' begins with the action of climbing. The 'H' is the ladder; the 'e' is effort put in to reach the place where communication can happen. The first 'l' is light ascending and the second 'l' is light descending, creating an exchange of energy between below and above. Ah, now the two legs of the Bear's stick look like the two l-s of the word 'Hello'. 'O' is the peaceful attitude of being open to an exchange with another Two-legged and indicates willingness to receive insight from the exchange. In this vision of the word 'Hello', the 'H' was yellow, the 'e' was white, the first 'l' was black, the second 'l' was yellow, and the 'o' was red.

The Colour Yellow

In our world, Time walks like us, with two legs, a step for day and a step for night, a vertical and a horizontal line, a standing up and a lying down, and it is again the seventh of the month, the day of the Fire Ceremony held to purify the many Oceans: terrestrial, galactic, universal, and also our individual and our collective minds.

Soon it will be the time for the first Sun Moon Dance in Scotland, and I am the person organising it. I woke up from a dream in which I was in a studio belonging to my Teacher. I wanted to touch up some yellow paint on an object that I had made. Looking around for yellow paint, I found a rectangular box with the word 'Annatto' written on the front and I knew that this was an expensive yellow paint with an exceptionally gorgeous colour. I stretched out my hand to pick it up, but I noticed that he was watching, and I thought: "Hum, he may not approve of me using his expensive paint." I looked for another yellow and I found a tube of acrylic paint which was the right colour. The paint in the tube was a bit dry so I walked over to where there was a little pot with liquid in. As I dipped the brush into it, I noticed a brass-coloured object immersed in the water, and, as I lifted my brush out, the surface of the water smoked. I thought: "Oh dear, perhaps this isn't water after all." Watching the smoke rising I backed off wondering if the liquid was going to burst into flames.

I woke from that dream. I came to meditate, and the colour Yellow was everywhere. Eventually it condensed into a yellow circle and as I approached, immersing myself in the intense vibration of the colour, I began to see a chick, a bright yellow Eaglet in a bright yellow cup-shaped nest. I did not remember the yellow Eagle I had seen previously being newly hatched, but it appeared obvious to me now that an Eagle which was yellow, indicating the beginning of something new, was most likely to be a hatchling. As I teetered on the edge of the eyrie, I heard: "To be eaten or to be the Eagle?"

'To be eaten' was indeed the colour Yellow and I would be absorbed into the Being-ness of the Eaglet and help it to grow or, crossing over an invisible divide, 'to be the Eagle' and this Eagle was already fully grown. I saw a thin Y-shaped Sun Moon Dance Tree and two feathers were hanging on the arms of the Y. I was surprised: "But feathers don't usually hang there, they hang on the horns of the Buffalo skull." I came back from my meditation thinking: "Those two Eagle feathers I picked up need to have loops added before the dance and I will do that."

At the time, I had no idea that I would Chief the Sun Moon Dance that I was organising. I thought my Teacher would be Chief, but, as it turned out, I became Sun Moon Dance Chief in Scotland. It was two years later at the third Sun Moon Dance in Scotland that, as Chief, I decided not to hang the skull of the Buffalo up on the Dance Tree, but to place it just outside the East gate touching Mother Earth. The Dance Tree was a beautiful Silver Birch. Freshly cut the year before, its stripped trunk had been creamy white for the dance to the South, now, weathered for a year, the trunk was black as we danced to honour the West. The two black Eagle feathers hung on the Tree, one on each arm of the Y. On the first day of the ceremony a strong wind came and twisted the feathers together so that, for the rest of the dance, they hung at right angles to each other in the shape of a perfect T. This showed me that in dancing we transcend Time.

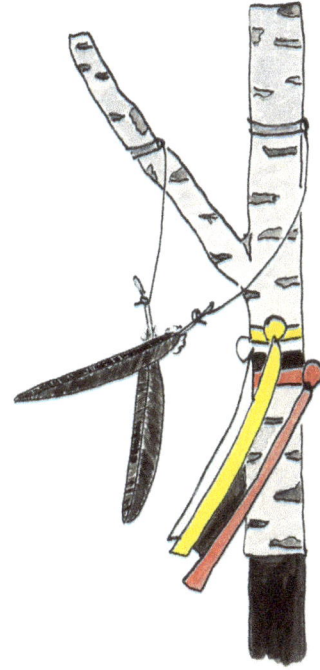

Tree of Time

Abouts

About Sixteen Years

Generally speaking, groups of people who are holding the Sun Moon Dance call dancers and helpers to the ceremony once a year. The first Year honours and draws on the power of the East. Moving clockwise round the medicine wheel, the annual Dance continues. The second year honours the South; the third year, the West. In the fourth year, the first cycle is completed in direction of the North.

On the following Year, the fifth dance to be held, a second circuit of the wheel begins at the East; the ninth dance begins the third circuit and a fourth follows.

A complete cycle of the Sun Moon Dance is 4 x 4-years, 16 Years.

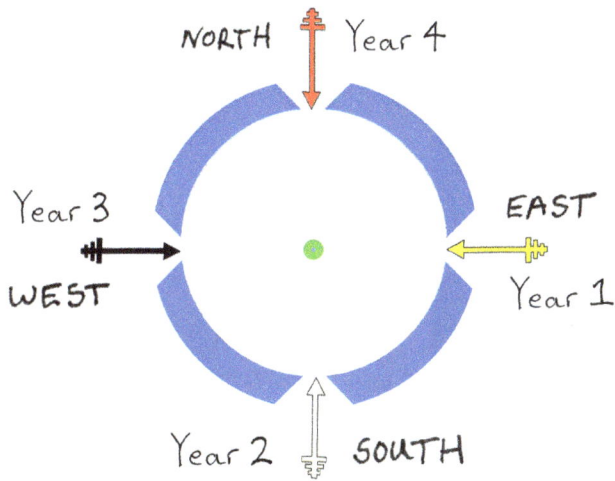

That is the metaphor of completion, and there are people, including myself, who have been at 16 dances or more. Whether an individual's contribution is at one dance or many, attending a Sun Moon Dance will surely benefit them and, as a result, our beautiful Planet.

About the Medicine Sphere in the Sun Moon Dance

At the centre of the ceremony, is a Tree. Set around the Tree is a circular area called the Arbour. At the compass points on the circumference there are 'Gates', one at each of the 4 cardinal directions, forming, by line of sight, an equal-armed cross.

During the ceremony, through these 4 gates, the powers of harmony, help, healing, and wholeness (the primal sounds of: -ah, -eh, -ii, -oh), pour in to enrich the world.

The powerlines of the 4 directions meet at the centre. From the East and from the West, day-light and night-light meet at the Tree; the colours are yellow and black. From the South and from the North, the physical bodies of water and the spiritual energies of fire meet at the Tree; the colours are white and red.

Perhaps, like the attractive force of gravity which pulls everything together to form a sphere, the 'Great Mystery' rests at that centre point, causing all things, within the sphere of influence, to be, simultaneously, both separate and connected, both individual and One.

In such a metaphor, the circle of the arbour is the horizontal plane of a perfect sphere and the form of the central Tree, where the original growth ring remains in the centre, holds the metaphor of the vertical plane, formed by Above and Below; the colours are blue and green. The dance arbour creates a meeting point for the 6 directions; a place and an opportunity designed to expand awareness.

Dancing their straight-line paths along the horizontal plane to and from the vertical Tree, the dancers' awareness of the all-embracing sphere grows. Carried by the Tree, they can reach out in all directions, encountering, along the way, the vast expanse their individual potential.

About Dancing Light

During the Sun Moon ceremony, each dancer is assigned a place on the arbour periphery. At their place they lie down to rest and to receive what they need. When a drum calls them, they stand up and, dancing to and from the Tree in the centre until the drumming stops, give, through movement, as much of their energy as they can. Maintaining the balance between 'receiving' and 'giving' plays a central role in the medicine of the ceremony and it is vital to the wellbeing of all life.

In giving their all, dancers create 'tracks of dancing light' which, through the repeated contact of their feet with the ground, soon become visible paths. As the dancers flood the horizontal plane with light, light from the vertical carries them; it is the Tree which is the conductor of the light exchanges. From the vibrating sphere of moving light that develops in the arbour, light streams out in all directions.

At dawn, in the rising of the Sun, the lifting power of light can be seen and felt when warming sunbeams carry the energies of inspiration, intuition, action, and transformation to the waking world.

Inspired by Joseph's medicine wheel teachings, here is an elemental story of travelling light: In the East, light, travelling in a straight line, passes freely through Air. In the South, light passing through the surface of Water is bent and travels on, gradually fading away. In the West, light, striking Earth, stops. Absorbed by growing plants, light ends its journey there. In the North, fed by those very plants, light dances in Fire.

The medicine wheel slows light and transforms it. Lovingly held within the metaphors of the Sun Moon Dance, dancers seeking transformation, also receive and give light.

About Drawing a Line

Of the 4 directional openings on the periphery of the arbour, 3 are the same width and 1, the East Gate, is double that width. This is for the practical reason that every person and every (other) material thing entering or leaving the arbour does so through this gate. But, as is always the case, the practical is inherently metaphorical and, to highlight this, a maize line is laid from the foot of the Tree at the centre of the arbour through the wide East Gate, dividing it in half, to a stone shrine placed some way outside the circle of the dancing area. The line is placed there to separate the 'comings-in' from the 'goings-out'. On a practical level, it avoids collisions; on a metaphoric level, it marks a boundary between the flows of energy. 'In' and 'out' flow in opposite directions, and drawing the line avoids entanglements.

This is one of the many metaphors that are built-in to the visible structure of the Sun Moon Dance ceremony, and there are other metaphors in the maize line that are not mentioned here. In this metaphoric strand, the presence of the maize line, draws attention to knots of all kinds; including those in the minds, the emotions, the physical bodies and the energy fields of the participants; all can be untangled and plaited into beauty in the dance. There is no need to think too much about the process or, even, have any knowledge of the metaphor: because it is made visible in the structure of the ceremony, it will have an effect.

The line of yellow maize; which should not be stepped over, which should not be overstepped; connects to a core teaching from Joseph Rael, first Chief of the Sun Moon Dance, on the creative power of Movement. In this instance, the contrary currents of 'coming in' and 'going out', just like the act of 'breathing in' and 'breathing out', are examples of the dynamic power generated by movement, a power that causes things to happen and creates Time.

Other Books by this Author

Tales of Two Coyotes: adventures with power animals

A great deal of fun and some profound suffering are the order of the day (and the night) in this book of 33 shamanic journeys taken while working with various groups of people in seminars led by my Teacher.

There are ten chapters in the book, each one introduced with a colour sketch.

On Trees

Leaving my 'safe' house and walking alone in remote places, I battle with my personal problems. It is a battle that occupies the majority of my attention but while I am engaged upon it, natural forces come in to play with my consciousness.

This book contains colour photos of the places and the birds that feature in the text.

Being of Earth

Loving the Buffalo from before I can remember, I am happy to travel through all times and all spaces in their company. I follow their wanderings until we come to the present moment: a place where the future is Green.

Colour sketches are included in the text as an aid to visualization.

The Messenger of Love

Stepping out of my cultural and social programming and overcoming fear, which is my very own, I manage to experience the help that is available beyond the world of everyday in a realm of consciousness where it is safe to be innocent like a child.

The book contains a light calendar and thirty-nine other colour sketches.

related websites: www.peacechamber.co.uk
www.somethingdoeshappen.co.uk
contact the author: stella@peacechamber.co.uk

Index

contents	images	page
	Eagle	
	the centre	ii
	sounds of the 5 directions	1
Divine Longing		1
A-ah		
	ah, washing with light	4
Feathers		4
	3 feathers on a shield	4
	T and Trilithon	8
	a familiar symbol	11
Flowers of the Rainbow		11
	7 flowers of the rainbow	15
Offering Myself		16
	8 energy centres	17
E-eh		
	eh, placement in eternity	18
The Heart Centre		18
	blue light in the heart	20
	3 feathers on a spear	21
	spirit levels	22
	in the blue	23
The Fisher		23
	crater and lake	25
At the Red Rock		25
	Uluru	29
	4 rock beings	30
I-ii		
	ii, awareness of self	32
Houses to Live in		32
	Drum View	34
Encountering the Power		35
The Eagle's Body		39
A House to Live In		46
	Fair View	51

Index

contents	images	page
O-oh		
	oh, returning to innocence	52
Being of Thunder		52
	Thunder Eagle	55
	the arrow	61
Becoming the Power		64
	entwined snakes	67
The Heart of the Father		78
	the heart of the father	79
	4 shelters	80
Be As You Are		81
U-uu		
	uu, carrying	84
Standing Together		84
	Dance Tree	91
The Rainbow		93
	Joseph in the rainbow	94
	the stick	96
	legs and feet	96
	the hole in the centre	97
	piled rainbow	97
	emanations from the centre	98
Time Steps		98
	Time steps	99
	Hello	101
The Colour Yellow		101
	Tree of Time	103
About 16 Years	Year cycle	i

www.ingramcontent.com/pod-product-compliance
Lightning Source LLC
Chambersburg PA
CBHW061730070526
44583CB00024B/3074